THE
GIRL'S
GUIDE
TO
Werewolves

BARB KARG,
author of The Girl's Guide to Vampires

adamsmedia

AVON, MASSACHUSETTS

Copyright © 2009 by F+W Media, Inc.
All rights reserved.
This book, or parts thereof, may not be reproduced in any
form without permission from the publisher; exceptions are
made for brief excerpts used in published reviews.

Published by
Adams Media, a division of F+W Media, Inc.
57 Littlefield Street, Avon, MA 02322. U.S.A.
www.adamsmedia.com

ISBN-10: 1-4405-0221-8
ISBN-13: 978-1-4405-0221-7

Printed in the United States of America.

J I H G F E D C B A

Library of Congress Cataloging-in-Publication Data
is available from the publisher.

*This book is available at quantity discounts for bulk purchases.
For information, please call 1-800-289-0963.*

For Piper Maru. Our life. Our love. Our eternal light.

For Mom and Pop for their lifelong love and support.

To Lon Chaney Jr., who in his legendary portrayal of long-suffering werewolf Lawrence Talbot when the autumn moon was bright, set the standard for all silver screen lycans. Their brilliant performances and transformations have truly given us a glimpse of the beast within us all.

And to Michael Sheen, the consummate modern-day lycan trailblazer whose absolutely stunning portrayal of Lucian truly reminds us of our humanity *and* our humility.

Acknowledgments

Let it be said that with all publications requiring intense historical study and research, this is most definitely *not* a singular pursuit. When the subject requires delving into a creature built more of legend than reality, the pursuit becomes even trickier. To that end, there are many individuals I'd like to thank for their gracious aid in pursing a rather hairy subject with a light-heartedness for which I am eternally grateful.

For starters, I'd like to thank Adams Media for their support and encouragement, especially editor Andrea Norville, developmental editor Katie Corcoran Lytle for her hard work and excellent sense of humor, and director of innovation and epitome of class, Paula Munier, whom I love more than Cabernet *and* chocolate. I'd also like to thank copy chief Casey Ebert, copy editor Renee Nicholls, layout artist and designer Elisabeth Lariviere, and proofreader Melanie Zimmerman for their swift and smart handling of *The Girl's Guide to Werewolves*.

Most importantly, I am, as always, indebted to my family, George and Trudi Karg, Chrissy, Glen, my twin nephews Ethan and Brady, and above all to my partner, Rick Sutherland, who is both my partner in crime and the love of my life. Likewise, I'm forever endeared to our close circle of friends and compadres, Ellen and Jim Weider, Jim V., the Scribe Tribe, Doc Bauman and his lovely gals who take such wonderful care of us and our kids, Dr. Richard Fox and his merry gang of amazing caregivers, and our beloved Blonde Bombshell. I'd like to give a special shout to my soul sisters Antje, Melissa, Judy, Kari, and my Gorgeous Sue for all of your support and the research you contributed. You guys are the best! A very special thanks also goes out to my dear friend and colleague Ellen Weider for her extraordinary expertise and research, Renee Downing for all her support, and especially to my *Twilight* expert, Ashley Arnold. You gals are the bomb! And lest I forget, the lights of our lives, Sasha, Harley, Mog, Jinks, Maya, Scout, Bug, Karma, Rayne, and especially Zeppie, Jazz, and Piper. I thank you all. I adore you all. I love you with all my heart.

Contents

Chapter 1

Who's Afraid of the Big Bad Wolf? 1

Chapter 2

Beasts of Burden 19

Chapter 3

Once Bitten, Twice Shy 35

Introduction

Welcome, dear ladies, to *The Girl's Guide to Werewolves*, a thorough presentation of everything you need to know about the ultimate untamed bad boys and their full moon escapades! No doubt, you have many questions about these big bad werewolves and she-beasts. How are they created? How have they evolved? Do they *always* transform by moonlight? Who came up with the concept? And most important, why do they have to be so darn hairy? Well, I'm happy to say that these important issues and many more are addressed so that by the next full moon you'll be ready for a night of supernatural werewolf-whomping!

While the concept of morphing from human to wolf sounds relatively simple, the process has evolved from a host of fascinating myths and legends, and I'll introduce you to them. You'll also hear tales of alleged "real life" werewolves, legendary lycans, shapeshifters of all kinds, and stories of Greek gods and moon monsters. Sound enticing? Well, that's just the tip of the wolfsbane, and trust me when I say that you'll be so mesmerized you'll forget about texting your girlfriends. Well . . . at least for a while.

Did you know, for example, that most cultures throughout history have werewolf sightings and superstitions? It's true. Together you and I will explore everything from the exceptionally cool tale of King Lycaon to the plague of European lycans during the nineteenth century to Wisconsin's infamous modern-day Beast of Bray Road. Forget Bigfoot, gals—this beast is the bomb!

In *The Girl's Guide to Werewolves*, you'll also learn how werewolves are created, how you can recognize one, what you can do to combat or cure a bothersome hound dog, and even how you can destroy one. Curses, magic salves, special wolfskin belts, and bad boys being, well, bad—it's all here in this dandy little tome. You'll also learn about different types of werewolves and how they make their spectacular transformations from human to mega-hound with canine savvy and major attitude. Do buffed-out bad boys with hearts of gold strike your fancy? I'm guessing that they do, and you'll have a blast learning more about how they cope with bristled tongues, moonlight madness, and *seriously* bad hair days. And be warned, if your boyfriend does happen to be a part-time werewolf, you may want to make sure your baubles are made of silver and that you've got plenty of mistletoe in your purse. No doubt you'll need it!

In addition to all the wonderful legends and lore, you'll love the mesmerizing tales that you can read and see in literature and films focusing on werewolves. In this book, I'll also introduce you to all types of lycan literature, from Guy Endore's 1933 novel *The Werewolf of Paris* to the fairytale world of *Little Red Riding Hood* to Stephenie Meyer's hunky Jacob Black in the *Twilight* saga. If that isn't enough to make your hair stand on end, you'll be howling in delight at the thorough two-part werewolf filmography I've included. You may not be aware of it, but cinema—from the 1913 silent film *The Werewolf* to Lon Chaney Jr.'s 1941 classic *The Wolf Man* to David Naughton in the 1981 horror comedy *An American Werewolf in London* to Michael Sheen in the mind-blowing *Underworld* trilogy—has helped dictate the majority of the traits and eccentricities we now associate with werewolves.

As with all discussions of werewolves, you'll find a wide range of stories that have taken on a life of their own. As with all things dubbed supernatural, this is a natural anomaly. For the purposes of this guide, I cover a wide variety of werewolves in their various incarnations, from the traditional "howl at the moon" werewolf to pop-culture hotties such as *Twilight's* resident lycan Jacob Black. To say that werewolves or the subject of lycanthropy is one-dimensional is a gross misstatement, as there exists an exceptional kaleidoscope of history, lore, and social underpinnings that play into werewolf legend. By reading this book it is hoped that you gain a well-rounded initiation into a world filled with light and dark and a huge gray area where you alone can decide if creatures of the night walk amongst us, watching and waiting and perhaps even hoping that we gain a new understanding of why they hunt, how they live, and how they survive—whether in real life or purely in our minds.

Enjoy the ride!

Barb Karg

Test Your Werewolf Knowledge

Before you immerse yourself in *The Girl's Guide to Werewolves*, let's test how much you know about werewolves. Please take a moment to answer the following questions and check out the answers to ascertain just how well you know your bad boys!

What is the most common way a werewolf is created?

    A. Being bitten by another werewolf
    B. Wearing a wolf pelt
    C. Being cursed
    D. Eating wolfsbane

Which werewolf film is based on the infamous real-life account of the Beast of Gévaudan?

    A. *An American Werewolf in London* (1981)
    B. *Brotherhood of the Wolf* (2001)
    C. *The Beast Must Die* (1974)
    D. *Teen Wolf* (1985)

If you were to become a werewolf, what are the first traits you would develop?

    A. The overwhelming urge to howl at the moon
    B. A heightened sense of sight, sound, and smell
    C. A change of appetite
    D. A sudden flea infestation

What's the easiest way to kill a werewolf?

A. Piercing their skin with anything made of pure silver, such as bullets, daggers, or even a cake knife!

B. Burning them at the stake

C. Injecting liquid wolfsbane or monkshood into their bloodstream

D. Using blessed religious implements such as a crucifix or holy water

What is the most common sign that an individual may be a werewolf?

A. They disappear during the nights of the full moon

B. They can hear the sound of leaves rustling from a mile away

C. If their skin is cut a tuft of fur may be visible

D. They refuse to eat garlic

The Beast of Bray Road is one of America's most enduring werewolf legends. The Beast has been known to:

A. Dart in front of startled travelers on a lonely road in rural Wisconsin

B. Has been sighted over seventy times, but has never been photographed or filmed

C. Attack sheep and goats in New Mexico and Texas

D. Resemble a werewolf with the head of a donkey

Answers

If you chose mostly A's: You have a well-rounded sense of the modern-day werewolf and many of the obvious traits and behaviors we associate with werewolves and lycanthropy. With that knowledge base, you will be very excited to dig deeper into the lycan mystique and learn even more!

If you chose mostly B's: Congratulations! You have an above average knowledge of werewolves in general. Even so, there's plenty more to learn about lycan lore, literature, and film—information that will pleasantly surprise you!

If you chose mostly C's: You're familiar with some aspects of werewolves and lycanthropy, but now you have the opportunity to learn even more as you delve into tales of alleged real-life werewolves and read all the inside scoop that showcases the best that ancient and modern-day lycanthropy has to offer.

If you chose mostly D's: You're going to have a blast learning all about werewolves, including lycan mythology, how individuals becomes werewolves, how you can combat untamed bad boys, and many other fascinating aspects of werewolfery.

Chapter 1

Who's Afraid of the Big Bad Wolf?

By and large, werewolves have been fictionalized and romanticized to an overwhelming extent. But along the way, many diligent researchers, fiction and nonfiction writers, historians, scholars, scientists, folklorists, and filmmakers have tackled the subject and presented a character full of history, mystery, romance, psychological impairment—and major attitude. That said, for the majority of folks, werewolves are nothing more than a myth. However, as with other legendary mysterious figures such as vampires, Big Foot, and the Loch Ness Monster, there remains the possibility that if something hasn't been clearly disproven, there *is* the possibility that it can indeed exist. Don't you think?

What Exactly *Is* a Werewolf?

So let's start from the top. What exactly *is* a werewolf? Among many answers, the easiest is that he or she is a person who's inflicted with a disease or curse and who, during certain times, like during a full moon, undergoes a transformation from human to wolf. Some werewolves maintain part of their human form, some become formidable two-legged howlers, and others morph into the type of wolf you'd find roaming the forest (see Chapter 4). But be warned. The one thing that holds true when it comes to all things related to werewolves is that their bite *is* worse than their bark.

Full Moon Madness

The werewolf is neither man nor wolf, but a satanic creature with the worst qualities of both.

—Warner Oland as Dr. Yogami in *Werewolf of London* (1935), trying to convince Dr. Glendon of the existence of werewolves

---

Lycan, Lupine, or *Loup-Garou*?

Embedded in werewolf mythology, lore, real-life accounts, literature and film are a wide range of terms used to describe werewolves, most of which are used throughout this guide. *Lycan* is perhaps the oldest reference; it evolves from Greek mythology and King Lycaon. *Lycanthropy* indicates an individual's transformation from human to wolf. Sometimes it's made in reference to the delusion a person has of becoming a werewolf, but it's more commonly used to refer to the werewolf affliction in general. Other colorful words such as *wolfism, wolfery, werewolfery, lupines, lunatics, lycanthropes, lycanthropia*, and the French *loup-garou* have also made their way into the standard werewolf lexicon.

In the Company of Wolves

The metaphor of the wolf is a powerful one that has been in existence since antiquity. Naturally, these metaphors of a voracious beast run counterpart to man's "inner beast" and extend to the werewolf and all measure of lycan myth, literature, and cinema. The fact that a lycan is half human and half wolf brings the best and worst of both species into sharper focus. Having survived the Ice Age, *wolves* or *canis lupus*, have been around for more than 300,000 years, which makes them the granddaddy of the domestic dog. In the wild, wolves are very much like humans in that they run in families, called *packs*; the females are highly maternal; and each pack has an alpha male leader. In general, wolves are very powerful and built for stamina, with strong chests and legs that can carry them up to speeds of forty miles per hour. Like man, they're highly intelligent creatures who fight for their survival and that of their families. If you were to choose an animal you could morph into, a wolf wouldn't be a bad choice, but as you'll soon learn, a blending of the species doesn't always result in the picture-perfect werewolf!

One important thing that needs to be discussed, given how much it's been brought up in the media, is the common misconception regarding which animals are part of the wolf family. The best example of this is the blockbuster *X-Men* franchise of films and the current release of the fourth film, *X-Men Origins: Wolverine*, which focuses on Hugh Jackman's wildly popular mutant character Wolverine. It's often misconstrued that Wolverine is a werewolf. Not so. Real wolverines are actually the largest members of the genus *mustela*—the weasel family. Badgers, or genus *mustelidae*, are a subgenus of that family. Unlike wolves, these animals are nocturnal predators who kill for sport rather than survival. Jackman's character—who is definitely *not* a werewolf—picks up characteristics and temperament from both the weasel and the badger, a fact accelerated by him being a creature built of human medical intervention. Jackman does, however, play one of the best cinematic werewolves to date in the 2004 blockbuster *Van Helsing* (see Chapters 9 and 10).

What's Up with the Moon?

The metaphor of the moon has been an integral part of human history *and* wolf history since the beginning of mankind. In ancient Greece, the first deity who represented the full moon was the benevolent goddess Selene. The moon's powers were later taken by the goddess and huntress Artemis, who also ruled the earth's forests and rivers. Although the moon's seemingly supernatural power was considered to be benevolent, and cycles of the moon were a known method for measuring time and planting crops, those cycles would develop a more sinister association with witches and especially werewolves during the Dark Ages.

On the Prowl

EVEN AS LATE as the early nineteenth century, the forces of the moon were often associated with frenzied or irrational behavior in humans. In fact, the description "lunatic" comes from the French *lune*, meaning the moon. Moonlight, it was held, had a certain influence on the human mind, robbing it of reason and allowing primordial passions and rages to come to the surface. What better connection to ferocious behavior than a full moon that could transform a seemingly cultured man into a ravening beast?

—Bob Curran, Irish author

Why did the full moon become a predictor of evil doings? By the light of the full moon it was possible to venture from the fireplace and into the forest, but the slight illumination created spooky shadows and vague images, and in some cases attracted nocturnal wolves on the hunt. Because of that, beliefs developed that only those who associated with dangerous beasts would dare to share the night with them. Another common belief was that witches and sorcerers would gather at the full moon to conjure evil deeds with werewolves who did their bidding. One of the first recorded descriptions relating the moon to werewolfery came from the English religious cleric Gervase of Tilbury in the 1200s, who wrote that: "We often see men changed into wolves at the turn of the moon." That assertion has since become a common theme in werewolf legend—and a fixture in fiction and film.

Multicultural Canines

Since the time of ancient man and across all cultures of the world there have been long-believed tales of men and woman who could transform themselves into wolves. In truth, those tales, with the aid of real-life accounts, literature, and film, have fueled the fires of lycanthropy and made it one of the centerpieces of the dark side of humanity and the modern-day horror genre. Part of our fascination with werewolves is due in no small part to their cultural evolution, which begins with the ancient Egyptians, Greeks, and Romans, where tales of animalistic beings permeate not only our dreams—but our worst nightmares.

Early werewolf mythologies and legends invariably involved gods, men, and creatures who held great power and commanded the awe and respect of mere mortals. Entire civilizations were based on the belief in gods who controlled every aspect of nature and the fate of mankind, and many of those gods held the visages of canine creatures. From those earliest beliefs sprang the mythologies and legends that compelled mere men and women to toe the religious line and do the bidding of leaders who, it was naturally assumed, had the closest connections to the gods or were even thought to be gods themselves. As civilizations evolved and religions became less dependent on fanciful creations, the power of werewolf legend and myth continued unabated. Many of those tales began focusing, not so much on spirituality and religion, but on things that most frightened people, who began keeping their doors and shutters locked up tight when the moon was bright.

Among the most ancient of human beliefs is the possibility, and very often even the probability, that supernatural relationships exist between mankind and the animal world. Today, the closest most of us usually get to actual wildlife consists of listening to birds twittering in trees or tossing a few crumbs to insistent squirrels at the local park. It may be difficult to imagine, but the populations of our earliest societies were far outnumbered by wildlife, and most communities eked out a simple living virtually surrounded by untamed creatures.

Although the majority of species in the animal kingdom seldom threatened early man, there were still a few competitive creatures that were near the top of the food chain. There's no doubt that these animals could pose a definite threat to life and limb, and very near the pinnacle was the majestic *canis lupus*—the wolf.

Anubis: The First Werewolf?

One of the first physical manifestations of man and beast occurred in ancient Egypt, and it was a pairing that formed a cornerstone of religion in one of history's most enduring civilizations—more than 3,000 years before the birth of Christianity. The "man/beast" in this instance is *Anubis*, the Egyptian god, who was thought to usher the dead safely into the afterlife. Anubis was generally depicted in statuary and artwork as a deity with the head of jackal and the body of a man, and he was so important to early Egyptians that every public procession was led by his likeness. Even the head embalmer who oversaw burial preparations wore a costume that displayed the head of the jackal.

Why is Anubis so important to werewolf mythology? Because he was the first incarnation of the idea that a man could be part human and part dog. In fact, many of the earliest examples of Anubis in ancient sculptures and paintings show him as a distinctly "werewolf-like" creature. Those works of art created a visual image that struck the imagination, and ultimately became the precursor of the man/wolf concept that followed centuries later.

The Lycans of Rome

Legend has it that twins Romulus and Remus founded one of the greatest civilizations known to man in 753 B.C. when they built the settlement of Rome on the Palatine Hill in Italy. According to mythology, Romulus and Remus were the sons of the god Mars and the priestess Rhea Silvia. Because of Silvia's status as a Vestal Virgin, she was forbidden to conceive children and the twins were ordered to be killed. Instead, a kindly servant set them adrift in the river Tiber, where they were found and rescued by the river god Tiberinus.

Perhaps one of the best-remembered parts of the legend is that the boys survived with the aid of a female wolf, which nursed them and kept them alive. As the boys grew older, Romulus and Remus built what would become the capitol of Rome, but after Remus made fun of the short height of the walls surrounding the city, Romulus angrily killed him and pronounced himself king, naming Rome after himself. The legend of Romulus and Remus helped cement the bond between man and wolf in world history, and the concept of being nursed and raised by wolves became an integral element of werewolf lore through the ages. Several films over the years have tapped into the famed twins, including *Legend of the Werewolf* and the *Harry Potter* series, which includes Professor Remus Lupin (see Chapter 7).

Going Greek!

The original legends of werewolfery were actually fine-tuned by the mythologies and historians of ancient Greece. Around 450 B.C., the Greek historian Herodotus—often considered to be the "Father of History"—wrote that the Neuri tribe, who lived in Europe near Scythia, would turn into wolves every nine years. The idea that the Neuri became wolves was considered more of a process of regeneration and rebirth than anything particularly frightening, but it helped set the stage for one of Greece's most enduring myths—and it was gruesome. The tale surrounds King Lycaon, and not only is it one of the first real werewolf stories, it also made *lycanthropy* a household word.

The Tale of King Lycaon

In Greek mythology, the primary god was Zeus, who ruled the lesser deities on Mount Olympus. One of those deities was Prometheus, who was said to have brazenly stolen fire from Zeus and given it to mortals. Although Zeus punished the upstart god for his rebellious behavior, many men began worshipping Prometheus and felt they owed him a great debt for giving them one of the necessities for life. One of those renegades was King Lycaon, who mocked Zeus and the rest of the deities outright. It wasn't long before the gods became fed up with his antics and haughty attempts to undermine their supreme authority. Assuming the form of a mortal, Zeus came to earth and began circulating among the people, convincing them that he was the true god and that they should begin worshipping him and the rest of the deities on Mount Olympus.

Hearing of this supposed mortal incarnation of Zeus, King Lycaon invited him to dinner to discuss the matter, and perhaps see what he would need to do to please Zeus. Of course, Lycaon intended to trick Zeus into the most unimaginable act possible—cannibalism. Lycaon had one of his prisoners murdered and used the body to prepare a stew for their meal. Smelling the meat (and smelling a rat as well), Zeus knew what Lycaon was up to and angrily blasted the dining hall with thunderbolts, shattering it to pieces. The frightened Lycaon attempted to flee, but in his rage Zeus cast a spell upon him, turning him into a vicious wolf as punishment for his evil ways. Unfortunately, Lycaon actually loved the idea of being a wolf and rampaged the countryside, gleefully killing everything in sight. According to myth, the people of Lycaon's land finally grew tired of the king's deadly transformation and eventually cast him out of the country never to be seen again. Lycaon and his horrific transformation became the namesake for the word *lycanthropos,* which has since become the basis for the technical term for lycanthropy worldwide.

Beware the Cynocephali!

King Lycaon's unfortunate encounter with the gods wasn't the only tale of transformation in Greece. Pliny the Elder, one of the most notable Greek writers in the first century, wrote a book titled *Natural History,* which described one of the most unusual species anyone had ever heard of. According to Pliny, this species were called the *cynocephali.* They allegedly lived in India and it was said they actually barked to communicate. Why the barking? Well, apparently they had the bodies of men with distinct dog or wolf heads! Pliny wrote that they lived in caves, wore animal skins, and used regular weapons like bows and swords. Surprisingly, the Greek physician Ctesias had also written about the cynocephali almost 500 years earlier, and Marco Polo wrote about them during his famous travels in the late 1200s. That's a long time for one legend, considering no one in India has ever seen the cynocephali.

Shapeshifting

While the earliest reports of werewolf-like creatures indicate that they came about as a result of natural birth or divine intervention, the most frightening idea is that they have the ability to change back and forth from human to wolf form. *Shapeshifting* has long been a mainstay of many elements of supernatural behavior, but in the case of werewolves the capacity to change isn't necessarily desired, and it can be a difficult problem for us mere mortals to undo.

Cry of the Norse

One of the most enduring mythologies in Scandinavian lore is the *Volsunga Saga*, which covers generations of the *Volsung* and *Giukings* families. According to historians, the most famous episodes of the saga suggest early werewolf transformation. In this tale, Sigmund and his nephew Sinfjofli stumble upon a house in the woods where they find two men sleeping with wolf pelts hanging over them. According to the lore, wearing wolf skins is a sign of bad intentions and is an indication of a "*skin-changer.*" Sigmund and Sinfjofli kill the men and then don the pelts to see what happens. Bad idea. Both men immediately change into wolves and—what's worse—they don't know how to change back!

After many days of wandering aimlessly and killing a number of men who hunt them in the process, Sigmund angrily attacks his nephew and nearly kills him in a fit of frustration. Distraught, he carries the badly hurt Sinfjofli back to the earthen lair they kept, cursing the wolf pelts all the way. There, Sigmund remembers an herbal remedy for severe injuries and applies some to his nephew's wounds. Miraculously, Sinfjofli heals immediately, and the two men are finally able to shed their skins and return to their normal human form. Wisely, they burn the pelts to ashes, and finally go on to have numerous wild adventures as humans once again.

Going Berserk!

Although the tale of Sigmund and Sinfjofli is just a small part of the Volsunga Saga, the idea that men could turn into wolves by wearing their pelts permeated Scandinavian culture, and the Norse Berserkers—a tribe of warriors—led the pack in creating fur-bearing fear and mayhem. According to legends, which were spread throughout most of the Scandinavian countries of Europe, far into the northern regions, and even through Iceland and Greenland, the Berserkers wore bearskins or wolf pelts into battle and assumed the animal rages of their kindred spirits while scaring the daylights out of their enemies.

Indeed, the Berserkers were thought to be so powerful and vicious, they didn't even bother with chain mail or armor and relied completely on their animal skins and generally cantankerous dispositions to get the job done.

Some modern theories indicate that many of the Berserkers drank themselves into rages the night before battle, and spiced up their drinks with a plant known as *bog myrtle*, which produced screeching hangovers and likely explains why they were in such foul moods upon awakening.

In a recounting of Iceland's *Egil's Saga*, the epic begins with the tale of *Ulfr*, who is known as *Kveldúlfr*, or "Evening Wolf." The wolf in this tale is a violent and ill-tempered man who, every evening, dons a wolf pelt and physically becomes a wolf to haunt and terrorize the countryside. Because of these tales, it's important to note that the concept of changing from man to wolf by wearing a wolf skin became enmeshed in the lore of Northern Europe, and it is still a staple of European werewolf lore and legend, despite the fact that it is rarely focused upon in modern fiction or film.

The Werewolf at Europe's Door

Like the vampire of legend, the concept of the werewolf probably wouldn't exist without the profound belief in man's capacity to change into some sort of demon—a belief that permeated virtually every culture and country in Europe for thousands of years. Many of the traits of werewolves were similar in all areas of the Old World, and tended to involve men of bad temperament and vile behavior, even in their human form. The primary differences in universal shapeshifting lore come from the question of whether or not the change is voluntary.

Northern European Lycans

Just like the rest of Europe, all of Northern Europe had their own versions of werewolves that differed only slightly, mainly in the names the shapeshifters were given. But no matter the moniker, the idea of the werewolf wasn't considered to be fanciful and mythical. It was just as real as any other denizen of the night and could scare or murder you just as easily. What follows is a list of werewolves of the north and the chilly countries they inhabited:

- Ihmissusi: the Finnish werewolf
- Kvelv-Ulf: the Icelandic werewolf
- Libahunt: the Estonian werewolf
- Varulv: the werewolf of Denmark, Norway, and Sweden
- Vilkatis: the Latvian werewolf
- Vilkolkis: the Lithuanian werewolf
- Weerwolf: the werewolf of Holland

Although lycan characteristics are similar in most countries, legend in Sweden suggests that women who own the fetal skin of an animal or who come under the curse of a witch will bear a child who's cursed. If the child is male it becomes a werewolf. If the baby is female it becomes a nightmare who haunts the dreams of those closest to her! Not a very good choice to make either way.

Eastern European Werewolves

Not to be outdone by their northern neighbors, the countries of Eastern Europe have their own rich histories of werewolves and their own names for them:

- Mardagayl: the Armenian werewolf
- Varcolac: the Romanian werewolf
- Vaukalak: the Belarussian werewolf
- Verfarkas: the Hungarian werewolf
- Vlkodlak: the werewolf of the Czech Republic
- Vourdalak: the Russian werewolf
- Vovkulaka: the Ukrainian werewolf
- Wilkolak: the Polish werewolf

It's interesting to note that the wolf-headed Neuri tribe, written about by the Greek historian Herodotus, may have lived in ancient regions of Poland, Belarus, and Ukraine. And, just as intriguing is the fact that the Neuri don't seem to fit into the werewolf legends of any of those countries. Still, most of the legends from these areas maintain that humans turn into the complete form of a wolf—not just halfway as the modern versions suggest.

One old Armenian fable refers to werewolves in the tale of a mother who was vexed by her young son, who continually snuck out of the house against her wishes. The mother said: "My son, there is a mardagayl [werewolf] outside." The stubborn boy slipped out anyway and spied an addled old man wandering about rolling his eyes and babbling. Thoroughly frightened, the boy ran back inside, crying: "You're right. I saw it!" From then on he minded his mother and stayed indoors.

Werewolves of the Balkan Peninsula

The countries of the Balkans, including the islands of Greece, which are just to the south of the Balkan Peninsula, have their own stories about and names for the werewolves that terrified their region, including the following:

- Kurtadam: the Turkish werewolf
- Lycanthropos: the Greek werewolf
- Oik: the Albanian werewolf
- Varkolak: the Bulgarian werewolf
- Volkodlak: the Slovenian werewolf
- Vrkolak: the Macedonian werewolf
- Vukodlak: the werewolf of Bosnia, Croatia, Montenegro, Serbia, and Yugoslavia

The vukodlak in Yugoslavia has become in many ways synonymous with vampires for their tendency to drink human blood. But the term *vukodlak* literally means "wolf's hair," and originally applied only to werewolves. Either version struck absolute terror into the populace. On a much different note, the *kurtadam* of Turkey was considered in lore to be a shaman or benevolent witch, who after very long and difficult spiritual rites could become a werewolf. Contrary to opinions of werewolves throughout the rest of Europe, the Turkish shamans who had the power to become a kurtadam were actually held in great respect.

The Lycans of Southern Europe

The werewolves of Southern Europe have instilled fear and terror for centuries, particularly in Italy and Spain, two countries that have created a delectable legacy that ignited the imaginations of numerous Italian and Spanish scriptwriters and filmmakers. These include:

* Hombre Lobo: the Spanish werewolf
* Lobishomen: the Portuguese werewolf
* Lupo Manero: the Italian werewolf

Both the Spanish and Portuguese werewolf legends made their way to the Americas, particularly South America, during early settlements that began soon after Christopher Columbus first discovered the New World in 1492. Lycan legends remain just as powerful and frightening there as they are in their home countries.

Western and Middle European Lycans

The werewolves of Western Europe may be among the most influential in legend, particularly those of French heritage as you'll learn in Chapter 2. French history is literally jam-packed with tales of wildly carnivorous canines, with some of the most enduring tales focusing on the fear and respect the common people had for the hairy combination of wolves and superstition. The two major culprits are truly the stuff legends are made of. They are:

- Loup-Garou: the French werewolf
- Werwolf: the German werewolf

The *loup-garou* is another European lycan that made its way to the New World through early settlements and became a permanent part of French-speaking legend. The German *werwolf* had an even creepier—although fictional—reincarnation toward the end of World War II. According to historians, there are vague reports of a desperate last-ditch effort by Nazi forces to infiltrate the Allied forces with English-speaking operatives called *werwolves*. Their supposed goal was to disrupt communications, assassinate important military targets, and initiate guerilla warfare behind Allied battle lines. Hitler was so convinced that Germany *couldn't* lose the war, he never officially sanctioned the idea and threatened to punish anyone who brought it up again. The werewolf and the subtext of Hitler's Nazi Germany play out in several of the most influential and best werewolf films, including the 1941 classic *The Wolf Man* and *Le Pacte des Loups* (aka *The Brotherhood of the Wolf*), which focuses on France's infamous Beast of Gévaudan (see Chapters 2 and 9).

On the Prowl

NEVER MOON A werewolf.

—**Mike Binder, American actor, director, and producer**

Canines of the British Isles

England has a limited history of werewolves, which is most likely attributed to the fact that the last wolf in the country was killed in the seventeenth century. But, despite that, local tales rear their ugly heads every now and again to keep folks from getting too complacent about the threat of legendary lupines.

In Wales during the eighteenth century, a wolflike creature the size of a horse was said to have marauded, killing livestock, dogs, and even men before disappearing into legend. There were three lycan creatures that were thought to stalk the British Isles, including the Irish *conriocht* or *faoladh*, the English *werewolf*, and the Scottish *wulver*.

Lycan legends are much more common in Ireland than in the rest of the British Isles. In fact, Ireland was so overrun with wolves that the Irish Wolfhound was purposely bred to help keep them under control. The wolfhounds were so important to controlling the rampant wolf population that it was deemed illegal by Lord Protector Oliver Cromwell to export them during the mid-1600s.

The Scottish *wulver* is unlike any other in werewolf lore. Jessie Saxby describes the wulver in the 1913 book *Shetland Traditional Lore* as being a man with a wolf's head who was covered with short brown fur. The wulver lived in a cave dug halfway up a hill and didn't harm anyone—as long as no one tried to harm him. It's said the wulver spent many long hours perched on a rock over the water known as "Wulver's Stane," and that it was very fond of fishing. The creature allegedly even left occasional gifts of fish on the windowsills of poor people.

New World Lupines

Legends of werewolves made their way to the New World shortly after the first establishments of French, Portuguese, and Spanish settlements, and as early as the time of the Conquistadors in the late 1400s in Mexico and South America. But the settlers weren't alone in their beliefs. Amid all the enchanting New World wildlife lurked a host of legends of werewolves, including the following:

- Chupacabra: the werewolf of the southern United States
- Hombre Lobo: the Mexican werewolf
- Lobizon: the Argentinean werewolf

- Loup-Garou: the French Acadian werewolf
- Skinwalker: the Native American werewolf

Just to keep things in the family, the *hombre lobo* is a direct descendant of the Spanish werewolf, and the *lobizon* is an off-shoot of the Portuguese *lobishomen*. The French *loup-garou* first made its way into Canada with fur traders and eventually traveled with the French Acadians into Louisiana, where it became a fixture in Cajun lore. Reports of the elusive *chupacabra*, which literally means "goat-sucker," first occurred in Puerto Rico in 1995 when eight sheep were discovered drained of blood with puncture wounds in their chests. Some witnesses described the creature as a small hairless bear with reptilian spikes down its back, while others reported seeing a distinctly werewolf-like creature.

Think the chupacabra is only a legend? Guess again. There have been numerous attacks attributed to similar bloodthirsty beasts over the past fifteen years in Chile, Mexico, Texas, and all the way up to Maine! The few alleged chupacabras killed by wary ranchers have turned out to be ill, emaciated, and mange-ridden coyotes. Regardless, the legend of the chupacabra lives on, and many folks believe the creature does indeed exist.

The Native American *skinwalker* is best known in Navajo culture as the physical manifestation of a witch who "goes on all fours." These witches generally used the pelts of animals they wished to become, an association that made the ownership and use of wolf pelts taboo. According to legend, skinwalkers were much feared and could allegedly emulate the sound of a child to lure their victims outside and into the night. Eerily, they were also thought to be able to read the minds of other men and could cast evil spells on their victims by placing curses on items of clothing, often causing sickness and eventual death. Skinwalkers very rarely committed physical attacks on their prey, preferring to work their evil deeds through sorcery and witchcraft. Needless to say, modern Navajos are reluctant to speak about skinwalkers and often debunk the idea as pure mythology.

Bark at the Moon

Although the legend and lore of werewolf behavior seems difficult to prove as fact, the reality is that virtually every culture has some sort of werewolf or type of were-animal presence, which makes it obvious that the concept was generally accepted by a huge number of people as truth instead of fiction. In the next chapter, we'll take a look at some of the specific stories and alleged real-life accounts that made lycans a permanent fixture in the minds of men, and firmly placed the beasts in the annals of horror history.

Chapter 2

Beasts of Burden

With all creatures associated with the dark side, including vampires, witches, warlocks, and zombies to name a few, there are plenty of historical accounts of folks and their interactions with these minions of the devil. Werewolves are no exception to that rule. In fact, with so many lycan sightings having been reported, especially in Europe, it does lead one to wonder, as with all things that go bump in the night, if in fact werewolves do indeed exist.

Hellhounds and Heresy

After exploring the appearance of the werewolf in mythology, you may be wondering why the populations of so many different countries believed—and still do in many cases—in the existence of werewolves. It turns out those folks had a lot of help forming their opinions, and it came from the most unlikely sources in early Christian beliefs and ancient religious lore. Though it sounds fantastic today, in antiquity it was generally accepted that the earth was flat. Even more frightening was the concept that lurking on the edges of the known world were demons, monsters, and werewolves, who were considered to be the incarnation of evil. As Christianity began spreading throughout Europe around 300 A.D., many lycan legends were actually incorporated into religious belief. Werewolf hysteria was even triggered during the Spanish Inquisition in the Middle Ages, when the idea that werewolves were the devil's children became a tenet of religion.

Sinners and Saints

The terrifying concept of werewolves during Europe's Dark Ages, around 400 A.D. to 1000 A.D., was actually somewhat countered by one of the most unusual legends of all. That legend involved one of the best-known and least understood saints in early Catholic doctrine—Saint Christopher, best known in religious lore for carrying the baby Jesus across a raging river and becoming the patron saint of travelers. In fact, the name *Christopher* actually means "Christ bearer."

Another interesting legend says that Saint Christopher was first seen in the form of a dog-headed cynocephali who was four cubits in height. That's an eighteen-foot-tall werewolf! It's said that Saint Christopher, who was known as *Reprebus* in his animal state, ate humans and barked, but he was unhappy with his horrific condition and prayed for change. Eventually his prayers were answered and, by converting to Christianity, Reprebus was miraculously transformed into human form and began preaching the faith.

Another version of Saint Christopher's wolfish appearance states that he was a godly, handsome man who prayed to be protected from the amorous advances of women. His prayers were also answered by his transformation to a man with a wolf-like head.

Although the image of Saint Christopher as having an animal form is generally unknown in the Western world, there are numerous paintings of him with his dog's head in many European abbeys and monasteries, and the legend remains one of the best-kept secrets in Eastern Orthodox lore. It's not often discussed, but we can surmise that film director and writer Robert Florey made the connection to this "secret" when he wrote the first treatment of *The Wolf Man* script. His lycan character is named Christoph (see Chapter 8).

Divine Agendas

The power of religion was so expansive during the Middle Ages that several intriguing legends developed suggesting that saints of the Church actually had the power to turn humans into wolves. In truth, it was a pretty clever way to usurp the power of the devil, witches, and a variety of demons by asserting saints could make such transformations. Saint Thomas Aquinas once wrote that: "All angels, good and bad have the power of transmutating our bodies." There was even some belief that Saint Patrick turned Vereticus, the king of Wales, into a wolf, and that Saint Natalis placed a curse on an Irish family condemning each individual to becoming a wolf for seven years. Adding further fuel to the fire during the early 1200s was the religious cleric Gervase of Tilbury's comment that: "We often see men changed into wolves at the turn of the moon," an assertion that has since become a common theme in werewolf legend.

Old World Lycans

The combination of werewolves in legend and religious teachings proved to be irresistible to European cultures, and stories manifested themselves in horrifying ways that were difficult to disprove—particularly when people started dying as a result. Accusations of werewolfery were just as deadly as those of devil worship and witchcraft, and it's often claimed that werewolf trials were nearly as common as witch trials in France during the sixteenth century. Even the infamous witch hunting handbook of the Inquisition, *The Malleus Malificarum* (*The Hammer Against Witches*), first published in 1486, noted the prevalence of werewolves, even going so far as to distinguish that there were two kinds of lycans—the voluntary and the involuntary. While the involuntary werewolf was considered to be a victim of witchcraft, voluntary maulers were considered to be the male counterpart to witches and attained their powers through sorcery and pacts with the devil. As you'll see with the following accounts of alleged werewolves, Germany and most assuredly France were especially plagued by hordes of lycanthropes.

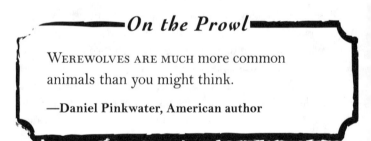

On the Prowl

WEREWOLVES ARE MUCH more common animals than you might think.

—**Daniel Pinkwater, American author**

The Wolves of Paris

Many lycan tales in traditional lore were jump-started by true stories of wolf packs attacking people. Those stories are all the more frightening when you consider that some of the worst ones took place not in the wilderness—but inside fortified cities. In Paris, hungry wolves made their way through the walls that surrounded the city during the winter of 1450 and killed more than forty people. The leader of that particularly nasty pack was an alpha wolf who earned the nickname *Cour-*

tad, or "Bobtail." Eventually, angry Parisians managed to lure the wolves into the heart of the city and overwhelmed the pack with a rain of stones and spears. But even after this alleged victory, hungry wolves just outside the walls continued haunting Paris for years to come.

Many historians have speculated that one of the reasons wolves seemed to be particularly hungry and aggressive in treating humans as prey was a result of the "Little Ice Age" in Europe that lasted from approximately 1400 to the mid-1800s. Winters during this time were extremely cold and bitter, and wolves were forced to search for food wherever they could find it. Another contributing factor to excessive wolf aggression was the Black Plague of the 1300s, when entire villages were abandoned and starving wolves went in search of corpses.

The Werewolf of Ansbach

One of the earliest documented stories of a suspected werewolf occurred in Ansbach, Germany, which was part of the Holy Roman Empire in 1685. During that year, villagers became alarmed when a wolf began preying on their livestock and eventually developed an appetite for attacking women and children who strayed into the forest. These frightful incidents began happening shortly after the death of the town's much-despised Bürgermeister, or mayor, and rumors flew that the wolf was a reincarnation of the wretched leader. At that point, the outraged townsmen hunted in the woods with dogs and drove the wolf out of the trees, where it jumped into a well in a vain effort to hide. Instead, the trapped wolf was quickly slain and the rejoicing locals promptly dressed the carcass in clothing, placed a wig and beard on its head, and actually put a mask resembling the Bürgermeister on its face! Satisfied with their revenge against the evil mayor and his wolfish return to the living, the people of Ansbach returned to their normal lives, and the attacks against the women and children ceased.

The Wolf of Magdeburg

One of Germany's most enduring werewolf legends was born in the town of Magdeburg, during the cruel winter months when wolves would often make their way into communities to search for food. In the early Middle Ages during a particularly bitter winter, small children began mysteriously disappearing at night, prompting the local magistrate, who was named Breber, to investigate. What was unsettling to Breber was that he could find only a single set of wolf tracks in the snow when there should have been many more. What was worse is that the creature seemed to be slipping into homes to steal the children away.

═══════ *On the Prowl* ═══════

SOME GREAT ANIMAL was lying on me and now licking my throat . . . Through my eyelashes I saw above me the two great flaming eyes of a gigantic wolf. Its sharp white teeth gleamed in the gaping red mouth, and I could feel its hot breath fierce and acrid upon me.

—**Bram Stoker, British author,
from *"Dracula's Guest"***

Even after Breber ordered a curfew and placed watchmen throughout the town, the predations not only continued—they grew more intense. Panic ensued when the child of a local attorney, and then the Lord Mayor's daughter, were lost to the prowlings of the unseen beast. Under pressure from the townspeople, and after his own angry wife refused to see him or speak to him, Breber began making midnight rounds through the streets of Magdeburg himself. As he was lighting his pipe in an alleyway, he was attacked by a cloaked creature, who turned out to be a crazed woman who had lost her mind after her child was killed by the mysterious nightcrawler. In her frenzied state, the woman babbled: "The night has teeth. The night has claws, and I have found them."

The addled woman led Breber through the gates of the city, across the fields, and deep into the forest. Much to his shock, he watched the woman as she gave a shout and began chasing a wolf with an infant in its jaws. Breber followed the chase to an abandoned hunting lodge, where he heard the snarls of a lycan and the screams of the bereft mother. Much to his horror, he entered to find the wolf-creature salivating over the slain and mutilated body of the woman and over the crying infant, who lay unhurt on the floor. Breber quickly drew his sword and thrust it through the breast of the beast, and then withdrew the blade to perform the final coup de grace by lopping off its head. But just as he swung his sword, Breber realized that the dying creature at his feet was no longer a wolf. It had transformed—and it was the body of his own wife!

In utter shock, Breber returned the infant to the townspeople of Magdeburg. He explained the supernatural source of the misery they'd all suffered and begged them to retrieve his slain wife and dispose of her body properly. The town burghers speculated that Breber's wife, who had accompanied Breber on a hunt the previous autumn, had taken a drink from an enchanted pool of water and come under an evil curse (see Chapter 3). The gripping Magdeburg tale of enchanted spells, love, loss, and ultimate death became a staple of lore throughout Europe and spread the fear of werewolfery, which quickly soared to new and believable heights.

The Beast of Gévaudan

When it comes to real-life accounts of werewolves, there's perhaps no story more famous than that of the creature who from 1764 to 1767 stalked the province of Gévaudan, high in the Margeride mountains of southern France. Descriptions of the beast from terrorized inhabitants who were lucky enough to escape its claws during the course of hundreds of attacks invariably insisted that this was no mere wolf. As a matter of record, it was said to have huge fangs, an enormous tail, and red fur that exuded a foul smell. If that wasn't enough, the beast was also said to be the size of a cow, and it could leap more than thirty feet in a single bound! With such an incredible and unlikely description, rumors ran rampant that the creature was a werewolf who was sent as punishment from God.

Amazingly, the first person the hellbeast attacked in 1764 was a woman who survived, after bulls she had been tending in the fields drove the alleged werewolf back into the forest. Unfortunately, one month later the horrendous apparition took its first victim, beginning a three-year reign of terror that earned it the name *la Bête Anthropophage du Gévaudan*, the Man-eating Beast of Gévaudan. In total, the formidable creature took over 100 lives, typically killing its victims by tearing out their throats. Another fifty people were seriously injured, and a handful of others escaped with their lives—and their necks—intact.

The now famous Beast of Gévaudan grew so notorious that in 1765, King Louis XV dispatched professional hunter Jean Vaumesle d'Enneval to solve the problem. Determined to serve the king, d'Enneval did manage to kill a number of wolves during massive organized hunts, with dogs and dozens of peasants beating the brush. And he actually took credit for slaying the creature itself. But he was dead wrong, and the killing continued unabated after he left the area. Finally, the king sent his own chief of the hunt, Francois Antoine, in a last-ditch effort to bring peace back to Gévaudan. Again, wolves were killed, and Antoine, just as d'Enneval had done, took credit for slaying the infamous beast. Like his predecessor, he too was wrong. The deadly attacks on dozens of people continued for the next two years until 1767, when a local hunter named Jean Chastel took part in a search for the beast and managed to bring down a massive wolf. Was this the *real* Beast of Gévaudan? No one knows for certain, but many locals insisted the beast was still a werewolf that had been killed in its animal form. Upon dissection, the wolf's stomach was said to have contained human remains, and the murderous attacks finally came to an end. A must-see adaptation of the story of the beast reached the silver screen with the 2001 film *Le Pacte des Loups* (*The Brotherhood of the Wolf*), a lush period film that stands as one of the best of the werewolf genre (see Chapter 9).

The Wolf of Soissons

Unfortunately for poor King Louis XV, the Beast of Gévaudan wasn't the only wolf at his door in 1765. The community of Soissons, a mere sixty miles from the king's palace in Paris, suffered a rash of attacks from a man-eating lycan that claimed four lives and injured fourteen more over a two-day period. The creature's bloody rampage began when a pregnant woman died in an attack. The wolf soon struck again only a few hundred yards away, leaving a mother and her son badly frightened, but alive.

The following day, the beast attacked a man and two boys who were badly injured, and quickly moved on to assault a man on horseback. As the man escaped to a nearby mill, the wolf gave chase and killed a teenaged boy. In a dizzying display of aggression, the wolf then killed another woman and injured several more hapless victims. Finally, a group of villagers gathered together and followed the bloodthirsty beast as it stormed through the countryside, killing and mutilating sheep and cattle.

The carnage didn't end until a local militiaman named Antoine Savarelle managed to pin the beast down with a pitchfork as a farmer dealt a final lethal blow. It's likely that having the Beast of Gévaudan very much on his mind made King Louis quite generous. He was so grateful for a resolution that he issued Antoine Savarelle a reward of 300 livre (silver pounds) for bringing down the deadly and dangerous menace.

The Wolves of Périgord

In 1766, a year after the Soissons wolf was slain, Southern France was again the scene of numerous deadly attacks. This time it was in the region of Périgord, where eighteen people were killed and many others wounded by a man-eating pack of

wolves. In this case, the citizens of Périgord banded together
to organize hunts, during which they vanquished a half-dozen
of the hellhounds in the forest. One of the most interesting
notes in this account is that an elderly man came to the rescue
of a hunter who ran out of ammunition during a hunt. The
brave old man used a billhook, which is shaped much like a
machete, to fend off the attacking horde. As in Soissons, King
Louis XV rewarded the elderly gent's heroism by giving him
an unknown quantity of silver and exempting his children from
military service. No doubt Louis was getting pretty tired of
werewolves by this time, and the French attacks were only just
getting started!

The Wolf of Sarlat

Amazingly, still another wolf roamed and rampaged
through France in 1766, but this time it was a single creature
who stood on its hind legs when it attacked. Even more disturbing were reports that the agile lycan attacked only grown
men and claimed seventeen victims during its bloody assaults.
Known as the *Wolf of Sarlat*, the creature was hunted by Dubex
de Descamps, the mayor of the village of Saint Julien, with a
party of 100 men. Even when pursued by so many during that
particular hunt, the Wolf of Sarlat managed to turn on his foes
and injure two of them. The hunting party finally trapped the
beast in a clearing in the forest, where Descamps slayed it with
a single shot just as the angry lycan charged for his throat.

Blood Moon Rising

While many of the famed European legends of bloodthirsty
werewolves suggest that the transformed individuals suffered
demonic possession with a tendency to mutilate their victims,
the stories of men who committed ghastly acts under the *guise*
of being werewolves further fueled the belief that the worst
bestial behavior was caused by the wickedness of individuals
alleged to be werewolves. There were also clear differences in

the way society tried to deal with suspected werewolves. In animal form, suspected werewolves were hunted by villagers and shot on sight whenever possible. In human form, individuals believed to be lycans were arrested and subjected to the will of the courts—which could prove to be just as deadly.

Gilles Garnier: The Hermit Lycan

Perhaps the most gruesome werewolf tale of the Middle Ages occurred in 1572 near the town of Dove, in the Franche-Comté Province of France near the German border. Just outside of town lived a hermit named Gilles Garnier—a particularly odd and belligerent man—who'd recently married and taken his bride to live with him in isolation. As it turned out, Garnier was accustomed to living in poverty, but he found it difficult to provide for another mouth to feed—that is, until he allegedly made a pact with the devil. Soon after Garnier made that pact, small children began disappearing, leaving behind only the vestiges of what were savage animal attacks. The locals suspected that there was a werewolf afoot, and authorities issued edicts to track it down.

Early one evening in the dim light, a group of workmen on their way home came upon what they at first thought was a wolf carrying the body of a child in its jaws. The sudden appearance of the men scared the creature off, causing it to drop its prey. The child turned out to be a little girl who was miraculously still alive, and as the men rushed her to safety several of them noted that the "wolf" bore an uncanny resemblance to Gilles Garnier. Reporting what they saw to the magistrate, orders were sent out and Garnier was quickly arrested. But what happened next shocked not only his captors, but all of Europe.

Clapped in chains and taken to trial, Garnier confessed to the murders of the children in chilling detail, but these were not ordinary murders. He explained that while he was searching for food one night, a ghostly being came to him and offered him a magical ointment that would allow him to change into a wolf in order to hunt more effectively. In his wolf form, he developed a taste for humans and began his deadly stalking and eventual attacks on innocent youngsters who played near the edge of the forest. Garnier was found guilty of lycanthropy and witchcraft, and the court was so horrified they didn't offer him the "mercy" of strangulation as a death sentence. Instead, they promptly burned him at the stake.

Peter and the Wolf

In Germany in 1589, the alleged lycanthropy of Peter Stubbe (also spelled *Stube*, *Stubb*, or *Stumpf*), the so-called *Werewolf of Cologne*, rocked the Old World with one of the most sensational werewolf trials in history. What added to Stubbe's notoriety and made his story even more spectacular was the 1590 publication of a sixteen-page pamphlet titled *A True Discourse Declaring the Damnable Life and Death of One Stubbe, Peter*, which spread throughout Europe a year after the trial and detailed Stubbe's grisly behavior in lurid detail.

Oddly, Peter Stubbe was a prosperous and respected farmer in his community. But little did his friends and neighbors know that like most killers, he lived a secret life with a much more menacing and wolfish side. Indeed, an excerpt from the pamphlet describes Stubbe's lycanthropy as follows:

> *The Devil, who saw him a fit instrument to perform mischief as a wicked fiend pleased with the desire of wrong and destruction, gave unto him a girdle which, being put around him, he was straight transformed into the likeness of a greedy, devouring wolf, strong and mighty, with eyes great and large, which in the night sparkled like unto brands of fire, a mouth great and wide, with most sharp and cruel teeth, a huge body and mighty paws. And no sooner should he put off the same girdle, but presently he should appear in his former shape, according to the proportion of a man, as if he had never been changed.*

With alleged wolf attacks near Cologne occurring with increasing frequency on humans, it wasn't long before the locals went on the hunt. Stubbe's evil incarnation as a werewolf, however, wasn't discovered until hunters with a pack of hounds cornered a wolf in the fields and then witnessed what appeared to be a miraculous transformation. The wolf suddenly turned into a man before their very eyes! Although this man claimed to be merely minding his own business, he was quickly arrested and taken before the magistrate for questioning. His answers were terrifying.

Relentlessly grilled, Stubbe admitted that he had practiced black magic since the age of twelve, and he claimed that the devil had given him a magical belt that would change him into a ravenous lupine. He also admitted that his first choice of prey was humans, and that over the course of twenty-five years, he'd voraciously attacked, killed, and mutilated sixteen people. Even worse, he also admitted to cannibalism. The German court was so appalled, Stubbe was condemned to the worst death they could inflict, after which his body was burned to ashes and his head impaled on a pole as a warning to anyone who might be foolish enough to consider embracing the ways of the werewolf.

Full Moon Madness

He has been bitten. Bitten by a werewolf. Now you will become that which you have hunted so passionately . . . May others be as passionate in their hunting of you.

—Shuler Hensley as Frankenstein's Monster in *Van Helsing* (2004), upon learning that Van Helsing is doomed to become a lycan

The French Skinwalker: Jean Grenier

In a case that was said to have signaled the end of the first wave of werewolf terror in France in 1603, the behavior of a fourteen-year-old boy named Jean Grenier turned into an unfathomable tale of horror. It seems that Grenier was fond of frightening young children with claims that he was a werewolf. Although locals who knew him thought that his stories were the imaginings of an addled child, Grenier's claims grew bolder and wilder as time went on. He actually began insisting that he'd been approached by the devil, who offered him a wolfskin cape and magic ointment that would turn him into a wolf for an hour on certain nights.

Grenier's outrageous assertions reached their apex one day when a girl tending to her sheep claimed she had been attacked by a wolflike creature. She said it was somewhat smaller than normal wolves, had a stump for a tail—and that it could *only* have been Jean Grenier! Upon questioning, Grenier happily admitted that he had indeed transformed into a wolf and that he'd been doing it for years with the help of his father and a neighbor. Both men were arrested and imprisoned, but after months of investigation the French courts finally concluded that Grenier was simply an incredibly disturbed boy.

Although Grenier concocted long and elaborate stories of his marauding and mayhem as a werewolf, no proof was found that anything he said was true. The courts found that Grenier had probably been in league with the devil, but they also felt that he was not beyond salvation. In a rare and lenient decision, Grenier was ordered to live out the rest of his life in anonymity in a French monastery, where it was hoped he would renounce his evil imaginings.

American Werewolves

By now, you're probably wondering about the werewolves that made their way to the New World from Europe. Not surprisingly, the effects of werewolf lore in Europe were developed in bits and pieces in American culture, although never to the same extent that they existed in the Old World. While the French and Spanish versions of werewolves, the loup-garou and the hombre lobo, struck the imaginations and fears of American descendents from both countries, the lycans from the rest of Europe failed to have much impact until modern incarnations made their way into twentieth-century fiction and film. Still, the concept of a man's ability to shift into animal form was a vital element of Native American belief, and it did indeed slink its way into some of the oldest legends in America.

Skinwalkers

The concept of *skinwalkers*, or *shapeshifters*, where men supernaturally change into animal form, is common in cultures worldwide, and particularly in Native American lore. One of the most common themes in popular legends is the man-to-wolf transformation. Among them are stories of the Mohawk, Lakota Sioux, Pawnee, Yaqui, Hopi, and Navajo tribes in America and the Nisga'a of British Columbia. Although some of these legends involve skinwalkers behaving as evil beings with ill intentions, most of them celebrate the connection between humans and natural animals. In many cases, the ability to shapeshift is developed through years of ritual and practice as a *shaman* or medicine man.

━━━━*On the Prowl*━━━━

YOU REALLY, HONESTLY don't mind if I morph into a giant dog?

—**Stephenie Meyer, American author**

Perhaps the most popular fictional literary version of the shapeshifting werewolf today is Stephenie Meyer's portrayal of Jacob Black as a member of the Quileute people in the popular *Twilight* series (see Chapter 7). Meyer based Black's tribe on the actual Quileute tribe in western Washington, which today numbers less than a thousand members. In this tribe's lore, the story of their creation relates that a spiritual "Transformer" came upon a wolf and changed it into a man, thereby creating the first member of the Quileute Nation. Native American skinwalking lore also figures prominently in renowned werewolf films such as the 1981 *Wolfen*, based on the 1978 novel by Whitley Streiber, and the 2006 film *Skinwalkers* (see Chapters 4, 9, and 12).

Beware the Beast of Bray Road!

One of the most bizarre legends of werewolfery in the United States began in 1991 near Elkhorn, Wisconsin, when a huge, wolflike creature walking and running on two legs began popping up in front of startled travelers on the desolate and rural Bray Road just outside of town. According to reporter and author Linda Godfrey, who worked at the local Walworth County newspaper, *The Week*, the first sighting of the Beast was met with skepticism, but it was a slow news week so she was assigned to check it out. Much to Godfrey's surprise, the stories told by witnesses sounded sincere, and as a result, Godfrey herself became a believer—though she's never seen the creature in person.

Since she first broke the story, Godfrey has learned of over seventy sightings of the bipedal creature roaming the countryside, and she has written two books describing her adventures. Fortunately for everyone involved, the Beast of Bray Road has never attacked or even attempted to harm anyone and has offered only brief glimpses of itself. You can check it out for yourself on Godfrey's website at *www.beastofbrayroad.com* or delve into the 2005 film *The Beast of Bray Road*, which questionably claims to be based on actual accounts with the now infamous werewolf.

Claws and Paws

As you've now learned, werewolves are all over the map when it comes to history, legend, and lore, and their prowlings and rampages have permeated the imaginations of countless generations. Now it's now time to find out just how these hairy creatures are created and the chilling transformations they endure as they become one of our favorite moonlight monsters.

Chapter 3

Once Bitten, Twice Shy

No doubt you're chomping at the bit to learn just how werewolves are created and what it would be like if you actually *were* one. I mean, how cool would it be to race through a forest unfettered by the normal trappings of humanity? For most folks, that enticement would be enough to make them want to embrace lycanthropy. However, as magical as the idea may appear, the werewolves of myth, legend, literature, and film aren't always gung ho about becoming midnight rovers.

How *Are* Werewolves Created?

Before you ponder the ups and downs of werewolfery, it's best to take a look at the harsh facts of how these creatures are created. From the contagious bites of infected lycans to the acts of pagan gods to deals with the devil, there are many legends that delve into the mysteries of how werewolves are made. Surprisingly, the concept of contagious bites became a standard only recently, thanks to the influence of films and books. From the deity perspective, only a true believer with a penchant for ancient religious dogma would actually go for the idea, but the concept that gods could turn unwilling humans into werewolves was an effective means of perpetuating the power of the gods and keeping the masses fearful and obedient. On the flipside, a deal with the devil could turn a willing minion into a frothing werewolf who could create more fur-bearing frenzy than the average mortal could even imagine. Let's look at some of the many ways it is believed that humans can get turned into werewolves.

Full Moon Madness

Dr. Vijay Alezais (played by Om Puri): I can't ask you to transform me with your passion, so I ask you to honor me with your bite. And I too will become a demon wolf.

Will Randall (played by Jack Nicholson): You'd rather be damned than die?

Dr. Alezais: Damnation is not a part of my system of beliefs. The demon wolf is not evil, unless the man he's bitten is evil. And it feels good to be a wolf, doesn't it? Power without guilt. Love without doubt.

—Dr. Vijay Alezais in *Wolf* (1994), telling Will Randall that he has a terminal illness and wishes to become a werewolf

Bite Me!

This may come as a huge surprise, but the *least* common method of wolfish transmogrification in myth and legend is to be bitten by a werewolf! Magic belts, wearing wolf pelts, curses, and drinking tainted water are mainstays of ancient werewolf mythology and real-life accounts. The truth is that somewhere along that lycanthropic course of evolution, getting bitten by a werewolf became a standard concept in modern lupine lore. Being bitten by a werewolf and turning into a raving lycan at the rise of the full moon is one of the more recent inventions of the imaginations of literary and cinematic writers in the horror genre. Repeated over and over in films and novels, being bitten or even scratched by a werewolf is now generally thought to be the number one way to spread the lycan infection.

Curses, Magic, and Getting Belted

One of the oldest traditions for werewolf transformations is the use of belts that have been cursed by sorcery or witchcraft. It's suggested in some legends that witches and sorcerers often wore belts made from wolf skins, or—even more creepy—the skin of a hanged man. These mystical belts could give practitioners of the evil arts the power to change innocent victims into werewolves who would willingly do their bidding and spread mayhem among the masses. While not particularly stylish, according to the tales, the belts did prove effective.

In one Polish legend, a witch with evil intentions could absolutely ruin a wedding by placing a belt made from human skin across the doorway leading to the wedding feast, an act that would turn both the bride and groom into wolves as they crossed the threshold. Only if the couple were given furs to wear as wedding gifts could they change back into human form, and that was only *after* they actually put them on. That certainly could put a dent in a honeymoon, wouldn't you say?

Born to Be Wild

If you happen to despise the curly hair you inherited from your great-grandma, keep in mind that in some legends, werewolfery is a hereditary trait, the result of a curse placed on a family line by a sorcerer, a demon, or even a man with religious influence. As mentioned in Chapter 2, Saint Natalis placed a spell on an Irish family, causing each of them to become a wolf for seven years before returning to human form. In Stephenie Meyer's *Twilight* series, several male members of the Quileute tribe possess a type of recessive werewolf gene that allows them to shapeshift into wolf form. The catch is that it takes the presence of vampires to bring out the ability (see Chapter 7). Whatever the case may be, it's unlikely that you'll have to research your family tree to determine if your ancestors were werewolves. Hopefully, a kindly aunt would have let you in on the ancestral secret by now!

The Chant of the Lycanthrope

One of the most unusual and perhaps frightening ways to become a werewolf in legend is to purposely perform ancient rituals to achieve a permanent extreme makeover. There are dozens of such rites, and without a doubt they would require a determined effort to achieve their ghastly goals. In one such legend, an individual wishing to become a werewolf scratched two large concentric circles, one inside the other, into bare ground and built a bonfire in the middle. Then he hung a cauldron filled with water over the fire, stirring in the seeds of poppies, hemlock, nightshade, henbane, and parsley to concoct an evil-smelling mixture. As the vile concoction simmered, the spell caster removed his clothing and inhaled the fumes while repeating this sinister incantation:

Hail, hail, great Wolf Spirit, hail
A boon I ask thee, mighty shade,
Within this circle I have made.

Make me a werewolf strong and bold,
The terror alike of young and old.

Through fervent repetition, the ritual was said to have gradually triggered a full transformation, as claws grew, fur sprouted, and the nose and teeth lengthened into the visage of a fearsomely frightening werewolf. Unless you really want to freak out your neighbors, it's not recommended that you actually try this in your own backyard. Anyone who finds you will likely put you in a muzzle, snap on a leash, and haul you off to the dog pound.

Don't Drink the Water!

One of the oldest-known ways of becoming a lycan is to drink water from the paw print of a wolf. In ancient European legends it's said that many thirsty travelers and hunters desperately fell prey to the lure of a small sip from the water-filled imprints that wolves left behind after a recent rain. Another perspective of the enchanted waters involves the wolflike monster *Grendel*, in the Old English poem *Beowulf*. In the poem, Grendel, who inhabits marshy, water-soaked regions, and his equally wolfish mother are said to be *brimwylf*—which literally means "water-wolf"—who guard the burial mounds of the marshland. In other legends, drinking water from a cursed spring or a stream that a werewolf had drunk from would pass the curse and cause an unwitting transformation. The best known of these tales is the legend of the Wolf of Magdeburg (see Chapter 2).

Salving the Savage Beast

It was thought that many of the werewolves of legend brought about their transformations by using ointments and salves with magical powers. Addled teenager Jean Grenier (whom we learned about in Chapter 2), as well as convicted lycanthropic killers Peter Stubbe and Giles Garnier, all claimed to have used magic ointments to bring about their transformation.

Full Moon Madness

I'm going to transform him, and unleash the savage instincts that lie hidden within . . . and then I'll be judged the benefactor. Mankind is on the verge of destroying itself. The only hope for the human race is to hurl it back into its primitive norm, to start all over again. What's one life compared to such a triumph?

—Whit Bissell as Dr. Alfred Brandon in *I Was a Teenage Werewolf* (1957)

Something Wicked This Way Comes

While many of the werewolves of legend were said to be innocent victims of supernatural misdeeds, there were others who were said to have transformed simply because they were naturally belligerent and prone to lascivious lifestyles. One of the first tales of a man who turned lycan just because he was ill-tempered was Iceland's Ulfr in *Egil's Saga*, who became a wolf every evening so he could rampage at will. The Norse Berserkers were also considered to be naturally mean-spirited, even before they donned their wolf pelts and went to war, and their legendary cruelty helped foster the concept that a hostile demeanor was necessary for lycan transformation. In modern literature, author Stephenie Meyer plays on the theme of temperament and shapeshifting in her *Twilight* series, where Jacob Black is given to involuntarily shifting into wolf form when he becomes angry (see Chapter 7). Even with men who possess normally mild mannerisms, there's little doubt that most werewolves develop a taste for mayhem—especially when the fur and fangs come out.

So You Want to Be a Werewolf?

Now that you've got the basic scoop on how the lycans of lore and legend became raging hellbeasts, it's a good time to stop and ask yourself a few questions before getting into the nitty-gritty about what being a werewolf is *really* like. For the average person, the thought of becoming a snarling man-beast or she-wolf may not be the most appealing thing the supernatural world has to offer. But on the plus side, you will have the freedom to reign supreme in your own territory with your own pack of canine buddies and see the world from an entirely different perspective, one that's free of materialistic constraints, curfews, and dating disasters.

On the flipside, becoming a werewolf is hard work. Depending on the type of lycan you are, you can face anything from painful physical transformations to blackouts to a *lot* of time in the pokey if you happen to prey on humans and are caught in the act. That said, let's take a moment to discuss what you can expect should you decide to become a creature of the night.

The Upside

As with becoming any cryptid creature—those creatures whose existence lacks scientific proof—there are very specific pros and cons you must take into consideration. For starters, if you decide to become a werewolf you will have a host of über-cool superpowers, not the least of which are exceptional vision, supreme hearing and smell, superhuman strength, and the outstanding ability to bop around a room fast enough to give Edward Cullen a run for his *Twilight* money. You won't be as pretty as Edward, and you'll have a ton of unruly hair to brush out, but you will be able to hear conversations from long distances and see Grandma's fresh-baked cherry pie cooling in the windowsill from a mile down the road. You'll also have full reign of the forest and all the amenities it has to offer. Truly running wild and free with little or no impediment will be the ultimate experience. Likewise, if you've always wanted to be part of a group, then running with a pack of wolves may be right up your alley.

Still one more thing to consider is your daily routine. If you're prone to being a night person, then you may indeed enjoy the midnight wanderings lycanthropy has to offer. Assuming you're the type of werewolf who turns only at the rise of the moon or simply at nightfall, then you too will become one of the elusive creatures of the night who can scamper about with little worry of being noticed by prying eyes.

Yet another set of perks is that you'll never again have to deal with bullies, being picked last for dodge ball, or dealing with telemarketers or persistent door-to-door sellers who happen to cross you when the moon is full. If you're at all uncertain about becoming a teenage werewolf, it's best you watch the 1985 Michael J. Fox film *Teen Wolf.* That right there should help answer of few crucial pubescent questions (see Chapters 9 and 10).

The Downside

As with all crucial decisions, there are always a host of considerations in regard to the downside of one's pending dilemma. What exactly are the downsides of becoming a werewolf, you ask? For starters, hair, hair, and more hair. And trust me when I say that it'll be sprouting profusely in places that hair should *never* sprout, and you'll have absolutely no control over it. No amount of Nair or repeated shaving is likely to get you off the hook and back into mainstream society. So be warned—that itsy bitsy bikini you've been eyeing is definitely *not* in your future if you become a werewolf.

As far as your daily routine, if you live with your family or you have too many nosy friends, you might not be able to get away with disappearing every month when the moon is at its brightest, assuming of course that you're the type of lycan who only turns at the full moon. If you're a werewolf who transforms automatically during times of stress or extreme anger, then you'll have a hard time hiding your affliction from loved ones. If cinematic and historical lycans tell us anything, it's that announcing to your family that you transform into a snarling werewolf will likely earn you a trip to the nearest lunatic asylum. So please think twice before outing yourself to your folks and friends.

Full Moon Madness

Andy McDermott (played by Tom Everett Scott): I didn't choose to become a werewolf. I can't face the fact that I've got to go around killing and eating people for the rest of my life.

Brad (played by Vince Vieluf): Better get used to it.

—From *An American Werewolf in Paris* (1997)

Along those lines, you must also consider your dietary habits. If you're a vegetarian, vegan, or on a strict macrobiotic diet, you'll no doubt have to give up your meat-free habits. After all, no self-respecting werewolf would be caught dead invading a carrot patch or busting into a vegetarian diner for a bowl of lentil soup. It just ain't gonna happen.

However, perhaps the biggest consideration in becoming a werewolf is that you would become what many folks perceive to be a dangerous animal. As a result you'll always be carefully watched and hunted—even more so if you're a werewolf who enjoys terrifying the neighborhood by snacking on local pets. If that's at all unclear, I recommend you watch the 2001 film *Ginger Snaps* to witness firsthand the result of what happens when lycans invade suburbia!

Howling Mad

So, now you have an idea of the ups and downs and ins and outs of how life might be if you became a werewolf, and the various legendary ways of achieving transformation. Let's take a closer look at some of the most important issues in the supernatural world of the lycan—how you can recognize a werewolf, which characteristics they may have, and which types of werewolves you are likely to encounter.

Chapter 4

Werewolf Characteristics

As a supernatural anomaly, werewolves are mysterious, engaging, and terrifying in their physique and temperament. And while they're basically predators that are intrinsically linked to man's "beast within," they must be admired for their intellect, self-preservation, and the sympathy they evoke for the terrible affliction they endure. With that in mind, it's only right that we give them their due by focusing on their superhuman traits and studying the various types of werewolves that people become. They're furry, they're fierce, and they're fully capable of either ripping out or stealing our hearts, so the more you know about these untamed bad boys the better!

A *Very* Hairy Situation

So let's get real for a moment. In Chapter 3, you learned all about the pros and cons of becoming a lunar lupine. Granted, the freedom that being a forest dweller provides along with the obvious benefits of heightened senses, strength, and agility make it all sound very glamorous. But when it comes right down to it, lycans are critters who, depending on the type they are, can be gnarly and intimidating and not nearly as exotic as, say, the average vampire. With that in mind, let's examine what makes the common werewolf tick, how they are classified, ways to combat them, and the possibility of finding a cure for lycanthropy.

Sights, Sounds, and Sniffs

The first human-to-wolf transitions that infected individuals notice are the senses of sight, sound, and smell. For most animals—especially wolves—the core senses are exponentially enhanced, a trait that can become utterly intoxicating to newbie werewolves. One of the best films to exhibit these particular perks is the 1994 movie *Wolf.* In this film, after being bitten by a wolf, Jack Nicholson's character, Will Randall, no longer needs his reading glasses, constantly sniffs the air to decipher all the intensified smells of his coworkers and surroundings, and becomes overwhelmed by the dozens of overlapping but distinct voices of colleagues in his office building. For a part-time lycan on the prowl, all of those things can really come in handy.

Buffed-Out Bad Boys

One of the few universal traits werewolves possess is some measure of superhuman strength, the extent of which runs the gamut throughout myth, legend, literature, and film. The Norse Berserkers were said to gain immeasurable and ferocious strength from the wolf pelts they wore during battles. In real-life accounts, individuals inflicted with lycanthropy were also said to have increased strength and agility. Assuming they weren't *real* werewolves, that behavior could be explained as excess adrenaline caused by a lycanthropic psychosis (see Chapter 5). Silver screen lycans have also been awarded all kinds of strength-related superpowers, from tossing an individual across the room with ease to effortlessly hopping across rooftops to performing all-out, computer-enhanced *Underworld* maneuvers. Suffice it to say that there aren't many wimpy werewolves!

Hungry like the Wolf

One of the distinct but inherent downfalls of the werewolf is its lust for not only animals—but also human flesh and blood. Given that werewolves are a reflection of man's metaphorical inner beast and that wolves in the wild are genetically preordained to kill for survival, this bloodlust is only natural. The trouble is, humans don't randomly slay other humans for food. Quite the conundrum for any werewolf, wouldn't you say? The key to being a successful lycan who can blend into normal society is the ability to curtail, or at the very least conceal, any human consumption. Some werewolves may opt instead to subsist on animals, some type of synthetic food substitute, or even herbal potions specially designed to quell the lycan transformation.

Hounds on the Hunt

The lycans of legend generally behaved as naturally as wolves in their hunting habits, and they usually sought out the weak and innocent who were foolish enough to wander into the edges of forests. Still, there are plenty of tales of brazen beasts who slipped silently into homes to steal away with their prey. One of the primary similarities between the werewolves of legend and those of fiction and film is their tendency to leave few witnesses or clues behind by leaping silently out of the darkness to dispatch lonely, unwitting victims. Another common trait of the cinematic werewolf, which began with *The Werewolf of London* in 1935, is that lupines have an unfortunate tendency to hunt and kill those they love the most.

Full Moon Madness

Rogan (played by Lance LeGault): What's it like when it comes over you? Would you know your own mother? Your parents—if they were alive, could you spare them?

Eric (played by John J. York): I'd like to think so.

—From *Werewolf* (1987)

The Good, the Bad, and the Downright Ugly

While we've discussed some of the concepts and characteristics of werewolfery that suggest a positive side, the majority of lupine issues are on the down low. Suffice to say, there are aspects of lycan idiosyncrasies that really *aren't* pretty! Among the unpleasant traits that are said to be part of the human form of a werewolf in legend are eyebrows that grow together in the middle, terrible body odor, hairy bristles that grow under the tongue, and wolf hair that grows on the inside of the skin. The idea of the wolf pelt just below the surface was exemplified in the film *Van Helsing*, in which both Van Helsing (Hugh Jackman) and Velkan Valerious (Will Kemp) transform into lycans by ripping off their human skin to reveal the werewolf underneath (see Chapters 9 and 10).

Bad Hair Days

Still another aspect of lycanthropy that most werewolves suffer from is *lycan fatigue* (a typical occurrence after a hard night of prowling). Another common trait is when werewolves are injured while in their wolf form, the bruises, gunshots, stab wounds, or any other affliction they suffer during their midnight prowlings also appear on their human body. Perhaps the most prevalent of the universal werewolf characteristics is what experts often refer to as *werewolf melancholy*. Most werewolves really do despise their curse and greatly suffer and regret their actions, most of which they feel they have absolutely no control over. While we explore the various types of lycans, bear this tendency in mind, as it's highly embedded in the overall werewolf mystique.

Altered States

For the most part, creatures of the night such as werewolves, vampires, witches, warlocks, zombies, and a wide range of genetic mutants gone horribly wrong don't want or ask for their affliction. Though they receive their dark gift through myriad ways—be it inherited, the result of a bite or curse, an intentionally inflicted virus, a death sentence, poison, science gone wrong, or a pact with the devil—individual critters approach their condition in unique ways. Much of that is dependent on the friends they're surrounded by, society in general, and whether or not they have a wise or an evil mentor to help them through the process of learning about what they've become. For most of these creatures in myth, legend, and both the literary and cinematic realms—especially werewolves—their character comes down to what kind of person they *really* are. A person who is good at heart and possesses a pure soul is going to be a much different lycan than one who's evil at heart and uses the affliction to chaotic ends.

In the lycan realm there are many types of werewolves and several classifications into which they fall, including *voluntary* or *reluctant*, and *avant-garde werewolves*. As with any attempt at classification, there are always those individuals who defy the odds and cross over several classifications. This is clearly evident in many lycan films, in which sometimes a beast retains much of its human form, such as maintaining facial expressions or walking on two legs, as opposed to only slight remnants of humanity.

There are also those who become totally mutant monsters while others simply become wolves such as you would see in the wild.

Voluntary Werewolves

Like many other historical creatures such as witches, vampires, and zombies, there are some lycans who, in their human form, absolutely embrace their condition and look forward to their transformation, abusing their powers and planning the mayhem they cause. The concept of a *voluntary werewolf*, however, is somewhat fluid in that its definition changes depending on whether you're discussing a lycan born of myth, legend, literature, or film. In lycan mythology, some individuals used wolf pelts in order to become wolves (see Chapter 1). The same holds true for many alleged werewolves throughout history, many of whom entered into pacts with the devil and were given a variety of articles, including capes, hats, wolf skin belts, and magic salves, that would instantly change them into a werewolf and allow them to succumb to their evil tendencies and attack or kill humans.

In many werewolf films we see a lot of voluntary werewolves who are hell-bent on evil, especially those consumed by revenge, those who serve an evil master, or those who simply cannot control their murderous impulses and show little or no remorse for them. The 2006 film *Skinwalkers* is a great example of the good versus evil lycan. In *Skinwalkers*, a lycan family lives a seemingly normal life save for the few nights each month when the moon is full. Instead of going on the prowl, they shackle themselves to a wall for the entire duration of their snarling transformations. The family also serves a higher and nobler purpose by protecting a young boy who is the key to eliminating all lycanthropy from the planet if he can live through an unusual "red moon" prophecy. Pursuing the boy and the lycan family is a pack of malevolent werewolves who will stop at nothing to make certain the boy is killed. That pack embraces its lycan transformations and has no compulsion or remorse in morphing and killing anyone who gets in their way (see Chapter 12).

Other werewolves are voluntary despite some measure of personal reluctance: They're willing to transform themselves into werewolves for the purpose of fighting off perceived enemies or protecting a loved one. Jacob Black, the Native American werewolf in Stephenie Meyer's *Twilight* saga, is a good example of this, as is Hugh Jackman in *Van Helsing* (see Chapters 9 and 10). Jackman's character, Gabriel Van Helsing, is bitten by a lycan and stubbornly fighting off the effects of becoming one himself, but he ultimately embraces and uses the condition to his advantage when he learns that the only thing that can kill Count Dracula is a werewolf who is of his own heart and mind and who has the will to fight him.

Full Moon Madness

Even a man who is pure in heart and says his prayers by night, may become a wolf when the wolfsbane blooms and the autumn moon is bright.

—From *The Wolf Man* (1941)

Yet another type of voluntary werewolf is derived from alleged real-life accounts. These lycans supposedly used their transformation not to leave a smattering of disembodied humanity across the countryside, but to hunt animals in order to feed their families or protect their livestock. According to accounts, some of these folks conjured up their inner beast to perform rituals that would improve weather conditions and help crops grow, an action that in many ways crosses into the realm of *white witchcraft*, meaning those witches who seek to do good.

The Reluctant Werewolf

Within the lycan realm there are arguably far more *reluctant werewolves* than any other type. The classic example is Lon Chaney Jr.'s character, Lawrence "Larry" Talbot, in Universal's *Wolf Man* films, which began in 1941 (see Chapters 8 and 9).

In many ways, Larry set the standard for the typically mis-understood, confused, frenzied, depressed, and utterly desperate werewolf who despises what he's become and spends all his time alternately searching for a cure or a way to die. Without a doubt, the original *Wolf Man* is a fully invested reluctant werewolf, which is a very important distinction because of the huge impact Larry Talbot had on all literary and cinematic werewolves. David Kessler, played by David Naughton in *An American Werewolf in London*, is another quintessential reluctant werewolf, as is Velkan Valerious (played by Will Kemp) in *Van Helsing* (see Chapters 9 and 10).

In addition, Larry Talbot brought front and center the issues of werewolf melancholia, suicidal tendency, public scorn, social deviancy no matter whether the individual is of the upper or lower classes, and lycanthropy as a psychological impairment—a beast of the mind and *not* of the physical world. Elements of these issues permeate the depictions of many future werewolves, from sisters Brigitte and Ginger Fitzgerald in the *Ginger Snaps* trilogy to Jack Nicholson in *Wolf.*

Full Moon Madness

Jean-Francois de Morangias (played by Vincent Cassel): So tell me sir, do they speak of the beast in Paris?

Grégoire de Fronsac (played by Samuel Le Bihan): Speak of it? They're already singing songs about it.

Geneviève de Morangias (played by Edith Scob): Instead of singing songs, they should be saying prayers.

—From *Le Pacte des Loups* also known as *Brotherhood of the Wolf* (2001)

Avant-Garde Werewolves

When attempting to classify werewolves, as with vampires or any other cryptid or classic movie monster, one must naturally take into consideration those who don't quite fit all the traditional standards. The perfect example of a werewolf who doesn't fit squarely into any category is the *Underworld* trilogy's lycan leader, Lucian, masterfully played by Michael Sheen (see Chapters 9 and 10). Lucian isn't bitten by a werewolf—he's born of lycan parents who are from the bloodline of William Corvinus, the father of all werewolves. So viral is William's blood that anyone whom he or his minions bite never reverts back to human form. Instead, the lycan form and utterly vicious killer propensities of William Corvinus's victims are permanent.

Lucian, as we come to learn in the third *Underworld* installment, *Rise of the Lycans*, is not only born human, but he also possesses infectious blood that doesn't cause permanent transformation. For all intents and purposes he's a lycan anomaly—one who early on transforms during the full moon, but with age learns to transform easily at will. So too does anyone descended of his bloodline. As far as lycans go, Lucian is a new species, and while he does possess aspects of both the voluntary and reluctant werewolf, his character is far more complex—which makes him one of the best lycans we've had the privilege of seeing.

It takes the perfect combination to build the perfect silver screen beast, which is perhaps why the werewolf genre isn't as flooded as the vampire market. But on occasion, we are introduced to avant-garde lycans, like Lucian, who stray off the beaten path. In many ways, Jack Nicholson also accomplishes that in *Wolf*. As Will Randall, he's yet another combination of voluntary and reluctant werewolf. What sets him apart is the spiritual and internal aspect of his character, which on many accounts stands as the antithesis of Chaney's reluctant werewolf. Randall, while consumed by the typical panic and confusion that lycanthropy brings, actually manages to approach the affliction from a more logical and practical standpoint. In the end, *what* he's become is more a matter of realizing what he can *be*, and for the lycan realm that's highly unusual.

Yet another offshoot pair of cinematic lycans are the Fitzgerald sisters in the *Ginger Snaps* trilogy. In these films, Ginger and younger sibling Brigitte are in a constant tug of war in their approaches to becoming hellish werewolves. Ultimately, Ginger falls prey to the intoxicating and addictive properties of lycanthropy and the social acceptance and power it provides. Brigitte, on the other hand, fights the curse with all of her might, always bearing in mind Ginger's fate and possible destruction, and ultimately her love for Ginger. What makes Brigitte utterly unique and rebellious in the lycan realm is that her devotion to Ginger actually causes her to intentionally infect herself with Ginger's blood, which is something you're much more likely to see in the vampire realm than the world of werewolves. Psychologically, this speaks to the pure essence of Brigitte's heart, in that she would willingly inflict such suffering upon herself. That action alone takes her a step beyond the typical voluntary werewolf. She's infected but she has no intention of losing control of her mortal form or senses.

Manic Morphers!

Throughout fiction and film we've seen a wide range of lycans and lycan transformations from the subtle to full-blown snarling beasts from the bowels of hell. What's interesting is that there are so many variations of metamorphoses. While many vampires have the luxury of turning into bats, rats, and wolves, lycans have only various stages of wolfery in their transition from human to canine. What follows are some general classifications of lycan transformations and mutations:

> *Mostly Human:* Lon Chaney Jr.'s Wolf Man, Paul Naschy's Count Waldemar Daninsky, Henry Hull's werewolf of London, and even Nicholson's lycan are common depictions of a werewolf that retains most of his or her human form. Typically, the changes that occur are to the head, arms, legs, and sometimes the chest. They sprout excessive hair, grow

fangs, exhibit some mutation to their nose (though usually not a full canine snout), and have glowing eyes. These lycans usually have heightened senses, adopt some aspects of animal movement, and show various levels of superhuman strength and agility.

Bipedal Werewolves: The term "bipedal werewolf" is commonly used to describe a werewolf that when in lycan form spends most of its time walking on its hind legs, although on occasion it will run on all four legs. This type of transformation can be the most painful and spectacular conversion to witness, as we typically see individuals change limb by limb. Their bones crack and elongate, a full canine snout and fangs warp their human features, and they sprout hair, which often sounds like a fire sizzling. Robert Picardo's impressive conversion in *The Howling* is an excellent and terrifying example of this type of conversion, as is David Naughton's initial transformation in *An American Werewolf in London*, though Naughton actually becomes a full-blown enormous black wolf during his final showdown (see Chapters 9 and 10).

Mostly Werewolf: These transformations fall in line with the bipedal werewolves, although there are notable exceptions to the rule. In *Underworld*, the lycans descended from William Corvinus are bipedal, but they usually run in wolf fashion. Those descended from Lucian's bloodline remain mostly bipedal. This type of transformation is also employed by Professor Remus Lupin in *Harry Potter and the Prisoner of Azkaban*. These transitions are usually fast, furious, and incredibly spectacular.

Entirely Canine: Total canine transformations do not result in the typical eight-foot-tall bipedal werewolf. These lycans make the transition directly from human to either a massive wolf or even a regular-sized wolf as seen in the wild. The film *Blood and Chocolate* accomplishes this in grand fashion. The werewolves leap into the air and their human forms are engulfed in bright light. Within that light, we see a very subtle transition from human form to canine form. By the time they reach the ground, they land as wolves (see Chapters 9 and 10). In the *Twilight* saga, the werewolves of Jacob Black's pack possess a similar capacity to supernaturally and almost instantly transform into their wolfish counterparts (see Chapter 7).

Mutated Maulers: For some unfortunate victims of lycanthropy, the transition is just downright ugly, and in film has proved to be alternately frightening or amusing. What these werewolves become is nothing that resembles a human. They also possess only partial wolf characteristics, which are often skeletal in nature and usually include an excessive amount of sticky slime or gooey drool. This type of fanged hellhound appears in the 2005 film *The Beast of Bray Road*, as the lycanthropic chupacabra in the campy 2005 goatfest *Mexican Werewolf in Texas*, and throughout the lycan transformations in *Ginger Snaps*.

Hair, There, and Everywhere!

Curing or combating werewolves is no easy effort. In the next chapter we focus on that aspect of lycanthropy and the varied medical conditions that have led some folks to believe they *are* werewolves. Of equal importance is an examination of the signs indicating lycanthropy. Would you be able to recognize a werewolf in its human form? If not, read on to find out what you need to look for and how you can protect yourself when confronted by a werewolf.

Chapter 5

Combating or Curing
a Beastly Bad Boy

A significant part of werewolf legend is how to cure them if you can and how to combat them if you can't! In this chapter we dive into how you would go about recognizing a werewolf if you came across one, and also the means of staving one off using silver or fire. In case you're looking for a cure for your own hairy affliction, you might be surprised to learn that you should be checked out for other things as well, as there are a host of lycanthropic medical conditions that humans can suffer from. Whether your medical insurance covers your checkup is entirely dependent on whether or not you bite your doctor!

How Do You Recognize a Werewolf?

Okay, so up to this point you've learned a lot about lycan traits and types. But how in the world would you go about recognizing a werewolf in order to help cure or combat his or her "ailment?" Perhaps the best way to begin this conversation is to outline some of the ways, both typical and atypical, that you can accomplish this task. The following issues and circumstances could indicate that a lycan is in your midst:

- You notice seemingly ordinary folks suddenly howling at inappropriate times.
- A friend cuts his arm and just visible under the skin you see a patch of fur.
- During a group outing at an ice cream parlor, you notice that when one of your girlfriends licks her ice cream cone, her tongue is bristled!
- Just under your teacher's shirt cuff or collar you see a rather large and fluffy abundance of hair.
- You catch your best friend eating raw meat.
- You mention to the delivery guy that your dad has a collection of silver bullets, and by the time you turn around, he's disappeared!
- At a slumber party, you mention that you're a cat person, and you hear a distinct growl from one of the guests.
- You give your great-auntie a pair of silver candlesticks for her birthday, but she refuses to handle them.
- The family cat and dog go ballistic and into attack mode when one of your dad's poker buddies shows up.
- During a full moon you notice the mailman's canine teeth start to grow and he quickly runs off, claiming to have a dentist appointment!

Now that you have a basic list you can fall back on, let's discuss the possible options you have when combating or attempting to cure a wolf in sheep's clothing.

Protection and Remedies

With the possibility of so many types of werewolves roaming the hinterlands, just how would you go about protecting yourself when the ultimate bad boy is at your door? Suffice it to say—it's not easy! While many lycans of lore are said to have succumbed to a well-placed shot from a musket or rifle, or to being skewered with a sharp sword, there were—and presumably still are—a number of wolfish beasts who require weapons with supernatural powers to bring them to bay. And then there are cinematic werewolves, many of whom are infinitely harder to kill than even vampires!

The Silver Bullet

Many of our modern methods for dealing with werewolves come from adaptations of the weaponry used in ancient European legends. The use of silver to combat werewolves began in German tales that first circulated in the early 1700s and were first published in the late 1800s. In these tales, such as the *Werewolf of Greifswald*, the *Werewolf of Hüsby*, and in the Brothers Grimm story of *The Two Brothers*, silver buttons from a hunter's jacket were loaded into a musket and fired into the witch or werewolf, causing her or him to admit or rectify any evil deeds.

Full Moon Madness

Silver bullets or fire, that's the only way to get rid of the damn things. They're worse than cockroaches.

—Dick Miller as the bookstore owner in *The Howling* (1981)

One of the common themes in these tales is that the buttons used were often made of *inherited silver*, which gave them a little extra edge in regard to supernatural ability. In other tales, the silver used as bullets could be as simple as coins fired out of a gun—as long as the items were inherited. The concept of silver weaponry was further solidified in the 1941 film *The Wolf Man*, in which werewolf Lawrence Talbot is finally brought to his demise when he is beaten with a silver-headed cane in the shape of a wolf's head.

The wielding of silver as a weapon against werewolves gradually evolved into the use of the precious metal in the form of any object that could be plunged into a lycan's body. These included a silver dinner knife used in the film *Blood and Chocolate*, and the silver cake knife that Christina Ricci's character, Ellie, finally used in the 2005 film *Cursed* to impale her fiendish werewolf boyfriend, Jake (see Chapter 12). In the 2003 film *Underworld*, vampire weapons experts developed unique bullets filled with liquid silver nitrate that rapidly invaded the lycan bloodstream with permanent and deadly results. Although many sources insist that the French Beast of Gévaudan was killed with a silver bullet, that claim is a fabrication that was introduced by fiction writers in the 1930s: It doesn't appear at all in French records or legend.

The Power of Herbs

In the lore of werewolf herbalism, there were a number of plants that warded off wolfish ways with mixed results. In the sequel to *The Wolf Man*, the 1943 film *Frankenstein Meets the Wolf Man*, poor Larry Talbot, who died in the first film, is resurrected by bumbling grave robbers who unwittingly remove branches of the *wolfsbane* plant that were placed all around his body to keep him in a state of unconsciousness. As it happens, wolfsbane (*aconitum lycoctonum*) is an age-old werewolf repellant from ancient lore—a poisonous plant that was named for its ability to fend off wolves and possessed individuals in their human form. In some early cultures, wolfsbane was hidden inside chunks of raw meat and left out for marauding wolves to devour, which was thought to be effective in sickening and eventually killing them.

Monkshood, also a member of the *aconitum* family, is another poisonous plant that has been used in regard to lycanthropy. In the first two *Ginger Snaps* films (see Chapters 9 and 10), younger sister Brigitte Fitzgerald boils down dried monkshood to use as an injectable, which does prove effective in quelling or possibly curing a lycan. Sadly, in the second film, Brigitte builds up a resistance to the concoction and is no longer able to fight off her transformation.

Among the most potent herbal lycan remedies are a number of common but poisonous plants that were thought to be effective in warding the wolf from the door. In addition to wolfsbane and monkshood, those include:

- *Henbane:* Sometimes called "stinking nightshade," *henbane* was used in combination with other plants to brew a toxic tea that could produce hallucinations in humans. Even in low doses, henbane can be deadly to all animals, including werewolves.
- *Mistletoe:* A parasitic plant that survives by attaching itself to trees, *mistletoe* has an ancient tradition in European culture as a folk remedy and is also used to ward off evil. Even though we still "kiss under the mistletoe," the plant is toxic and can be lethal.
- *Mountain Ash:* Sometimes called the "European rowan," *mountain ash* is a medium-sized tree that has been prized for its beauty for centuries. Because the bark, fruit, and lovely white blooms are attractive to wildlife such as deer, rabbits, and birds, mountain ash was thought to be a natural deterrent to evil and was often planted close to homes to keep both vampires and werewolves at bay.
- *Nightshade:* Often referred to as "belladonna" and "deadly nightshade," *nightshade* is one of the most toxic plants known to man, and was often used as a poison by the ancient Romans. Nightshade is particularly dangerous because the leaves are attractive and taste slightly sweet, but eating a single leaf can kill a grown man—or even a werewolf.

A Ragtag Bag of Remedies

One of the primary differences between lycans and their vampire counterparts is that religious artifacts such as crucifixes and holy water have little or no effect on werewolves. Regardless, in early lore it was thought that exorcisms performed by priests could bring an end to virtually any demonic possession, including werewolfery. Spiritual and religious healers also felt that forcing suspected werewolves to endure intense physical exhaustion was enough to bring an end to their wolfish ways. Another common curative, which was especially prevalent in the cases of pagan werewolves, was to convert the heathen werewolf to Christianity. Ultimately, according to modern lore and legacy, it's fire or the tried and true silver bullet that can kill a werewolf. Other than that, it's probably best to run like the wind and don't look back!

Is He *Really* a Werewolf?

Before you go blasting silver-tipped holes into every hairy guy who crosses your path, I had better point out that the rabid "werewolf" you ran into on the street might be someone who's having a bad day, has a medical disorder, or has just had a bad sandwich. How's that possible, you ask?

Catcher in the Rye

One explanation for the werewolf phenomena in the Middle Ages is the theory that peasants who relied on wheat and rye may have used grains infected with a fungus known as *ergot*. This nasty little fungus can cause severe hallucinations and alter perceptions to the point that those who eat it can imagine they've become animals or that they're seeing other folks make beastly transformations. In one recorded case in 1951, nearly 130 townspeople of Pont-Saint-Esprit, France, ate bread infected with ergot and had psychotic visions of being attacked by wild creatures and turning into beasts.

Doggy Diseases

From the medical perspective there are actually a few disorders that can create the image of wolfishness. Although extremely rare, the genetic trait of *porphyria* can produce severe light sensitivity that makes daylight extremely unpleasant. Left untreated it can cause skin discoloration, excessive growth of body hair, and deterioration of the skin, teeth, and fingernails. Porphyria can eventually lead to delirium and manic behavior that can turn anyone afflicted with it into one sick puppy. Sometimes linked as a possible cause of lycanthropy, it's also often mentioned as a cause of vampirism.

Two other medical mysteries often associated with werewolfery are *hypertrichosis* and *rabies*. Hypertrichosis causes extreme hair growth all over the body. In very rare cases, individuals suffering from hypertrichosis can develop furry bodies and faces that literally give them the appearance of a werewolf. If you've seen photographs of men, women, or children sporting excessive hair, it's likely you've seen some of the folks suffering from the disease, many of whom appeared in circuses and traveling sideshows, typically as part of a freak show.

On the Prowl

[DOM JUAN] BELIEVES neither in Heaven, nor the saints, nor God, nor the Werewolf.

—Molière, French comic playwright

Rabies is probably the most commonly known of these werewolf-like diseases. Although rabies seldom affects people today, it was much more common in ancient times. People bitten by rabid animals were quickly afflicted and suffered severe mental confusion, paranoia, and abnormal behavior. The latter stages of the disease resulted in a ghastly foaming at the mouth caused by excessive saliva production, muscle contractions, and then a slow and painful death.

The Clinical Lycan

Clinical lycanthropy is a rare psychological disorder in which sufferers are convinced that they are, or occasionally become, animals and often behave accordingly by skulking about and growling. This type of belief and behavior is generally considered to be a byproduct of schizophrenia, bipolar disorder, or severe depression.

On the Prowl

MIDNIGHT, AND THE clock strikes. It is Christmas Day, the werewolves' birthday, the door of the solstice still wide enough open to let them all slink through.

—Angela Carter, British novelist

In the *Encyclopedia of the Undead: A Field Guide to the Creatures That Cannot Rest in Peace*, esteemed author Dr. Bob Curran tells of a patient whom Sigmund Freud treated in 1914. Nicknamed the "Wolf Man," he was a Russian male in his late twenties who suffered from having excessively vivid dreams about wolves. What made this particular man's trauma so interesting is the fact that not only was he born on December 25—a sure sign in folklore that he was doomed—but also he had a membrane across his face called a *caul*, which is another common sign relating to witches, vampires, and lycans. Oftentimes, the superstitious aspects of lycanthropy don't appear in werewolf cinema, but this particular superstition plays a big part in the 1961 Hammer film *The Curse of the Werewolf* and the 1975 film *Legend of the Werewolf,* both of which were based on Guy Endore's 1933 novel *The Werewolf of Paris,* which also highlighted the alleged doom of being born on Christmas Eve (see Chapters 6 and 11).

Getting Hysterical

Another possible connection between mental mind games and lycanthropy involves *mass hysteria* or *mass contagion,* in which entire groups of people who are fearful and under stress often behave in bizarre ways and begin imagining events that aren't based in reality. Some form of mass hysteria has been credited with triggering the Salem witch trials in 1692 and the Spanish Inquisition during the Middle Ages. Both events resulted in conjuring extreme paranoia, and individuals suddenly believed they were encountering possessed demons around every corner. Many historical researchers have estimated that between the early 1500s and 1600s in France there were 30,000 trials conducted for suspected werewolves—trials likely sensationalized as a result of mass hysteria.

Furry Fiction

So, you might be pondering how the werewolves we've come to love and loathe have become such a huge part of the horror scene—creatures that have even managed to slink their way into our romantic mindset. Although some of the most memorable werewolves have easily been the mainstays of classic lupine cinema, it was the work of several creative authors who contributed to bringing the werewolf to life in our imaginations. In the next chapter, we'll take a look at some of the early forays into lupine literature, and we'll see just how they've evolved into some of the coolest characters ever created.

Chapter 6

The Early Literary Lycan

There's little question that our love affair with werewolves wouldn't exist without the creative license and lupine-obsessed imaginations of writers during the early 1900s. From some of the first children's stories to offerings from more recent writers of the last two decades, werewolves have evolved into some of the fiercest foes and romantic rogues to ever see the light of day—or even the mysterious mask of moonlit mayhem.

Early Writings of Lunar Lupines

Over the years, the werewolf has become a staple of horror fiction, fantasy, science fiction, and romance. Prior to the invention of the printing press in 1440, scribes, scholars, and monks spent years developing the long forgotten craft of handwriting volumes of literature into painstakingly recreated historically significant books with alleged real-life accounts of werewolves that have miraculously survived the ages. Without their efforts, we would know little of the earliest lore and mythologies that have made the werewolf legend a mainstay of modern entertainment.

Assyrian Tragedies

Perhaps the earliest man-to-wolf transformation on record is contained in the *Epic of Gilgamesh*, one of the first literary works in history. It may be difficult to comprehend just how old this text is, but the written epic dates back to 700 B.C., and it still exists today in twelve clay tablets written in cuneiform characters in the ancient Akkadian language—one of the original written forms of communication known to mankind. The texts were first discovered in what is now Iraq by English archaeologist Austen Henry Layard in the mid-1840s, and they are part of an enormous collection of almost 40,000 tablets in the collection of the British Museum. That priceless collection, which was created by Assyrian king Ashurnbanipal in 600 B.C., is part of the oldest library in the world.

The *Epic of Gilgamesh*, which first originated in late 2000 B.C., relates the story of the goddess Ishtar who falls in love with Gilgamesh, who's part god and part human. Ishtar believes Gilgamesh to be a hero and professes her love to him, but Gilgamesh rebukes her by listing the number of men she's claimed to love and the horrible spells she's cast upon them. On that list is the "master herdsman," who had dutifully baked bread and slaughtered a lamb for Ishtar every day. The fickle Ishtar cruelly repaid the herdsman's devotion by turning him into a wolf so his own shepherds and dogs would chase him and snap at his heels. According to the tale, Ishtar is so furious with Gilgamesh's cheeky response she releases the "Bull of Heaven," who would bring a seven-year famine to the world. Fortunately, Gilgamesh destroys the bull in battle, saving mankind and frustrating Ishtar's evil plan.

Full Moon Madness

Van Helsing (played by Hugh Jackman): Why does Dracula have a cure?

Carl (played by David Wenham): Because the only thing that can kill him is a werewolf.

Anna Valerious (played by Kate Beckinsale): But Dracula has been using werewolves to do his bidding for centuries.

Carl: Yes, but if one ever had the will to turn on him he'd need a cure to remove the curse and make him human before it bit him.

—Discussing the ultimate torment of the voluntary werewolf after learning Dracula has a cure for lycanthropy in *Van Helsing* (2004)

Ovid and the First Lycanthrope

In the Roman world at the beginning of the first century, the poet Ovid made werewolf history by writing the Greek myth of King Lycaon in the poetic text of *Metamorphoses*, which was first published in 8 A.D. The tale of Lycaon, who was transformed into a wolf by the god Zeus after trying to trick the deity into eating flesh, was among many in the book that depicted supernatural transformations (see Chapter 1). Unfortunately, no original manuscripts of Ovid's works exist today, and the oldest complete text dates to 1100 A.D. Ovid's *Metamorphoses* was an immediate success with the literate Roman population who admired his work, and the book has remained a classic of literature. Interestingly, the content of *Metamorphoses* did experience a very real threat in the late Middle Ages when the Catholic Church deemed the book a "dangerously pagan work." A transformation-free version of the poem was eventually published and also proved to be immensely popular. Ovid's tale of Lycaon, however, has survived to become the basis for the term *lycanthropy* as we know and love it today.

Romantic Medieval Werewolves

In medieval England in 1175, a French woman known only by the name Marie wrote *The Lais of Marie de France*, a series of twelve poems that exemplified the glories of courtly love. One of those poems concerned the tragic but fascinating tale of *Bisclavret*, a British lord whose wife betrays him after discovering he is a werewolf. The poem was the first popular work that portrayed werewolves in a benevolent light, a classic theme that has been retold countless times in modified versions and that inspired lyrical lupine poetry to follow.

On the Prowl

WOLVES DO CHANGE their hair, but not their heart.

—Ben Jonson, British poet and playwright

According to Marie's poem, Bisclavret mysteriously disappears every week for three days, and after much begging and pleading from his wife, he finally confesses that he's a werewolf. Bisclavret also tells her that before he transforms, he must remove his clothes and hide them beneath a bush next to a large rock by the chapel near their estate. After three days of living and hunting as a wolf he must return to the hiding place to regain his clothing or else he will be cursed to remain a wolf forever.

Disturbed by this news, Bisclavret's wife begins plotting. She wickedly takes a knight as her lover and convinces him to sneak out to Bisclavret's hiding place and steal his clothing while he is out hunting. This condemns Bisclavret to a life of wolfery and frees her to remarry and procure his lands and wealth. The wife accomplishes her evil ploy and Bisclavret is forced to live for a year in the wild until the king discovers him while hunting with his dogs. When the "wolf" approaches the king's horse and grasps the stirrup to kiss his foot, the king realizes that this is no wild creature and takes him in as a faithful companion.

After much time in the king's court, Bisclavret spies and tries to attack the knight who helped betray him. Later, at one of the king's banquets, Bisclavret springs upon his unfaithful wife and manages to bite off her nose. The king's wise counselor insists that there must certainly be a good reason for the wolf's sudden and vicious assaults that were aimed exclusively at these two individuals, because Bisclavret has been such a gentle and faithful companion to the king. Under torture, both the wife and the knight confess to their crime and are forced to return the stolen clothing, whereupon Bisclavret resumes his human form and the king restores his rightful property. What became of the deceitful wife and knight, you ask? They were banished from the country, and it is said that their daughters were born without noses!

The Romance of Guillaume de Palerme

Another poem of the Middle Ages that depicts werewolves in a kindly light was composed in France around A.D. 1200 as a commissioned work by an unknown author for Countess Yolande of Flanders in Belgium. An English version of the poem was re-created in 1350 by a poet known only as William, and the sole surviving manuscript of his work is held at King's

College in Cambridge, England. The tale recounts the adventures of *Guillaume de Palerme*, who has his inheritance stolen by a murderous uncle. Guillaume escapes from his deceitful uncle and is aided by the benevolent werewolf Alfonso, who turns out to be the victim of a spell cast by his stepmother. In human form, Alfonso is actually a prince and the son of the King of Spain. After numerous adventures, Guillaume meets and marries Melior, a princess of Rome, and regains his inheritance. Alfonso's story ends happily after the werewolf spell is broken as he falls in love with Guillaume's sister and marries her as well. Unfortunately, many of the werewolf tales to follow would not have such perfect fairytale endings.

Fairytale Fiends

Among the original tales of lycans on the printed page, children's fairytales are a source of some of the earliest wolfish works of fiction. In the original versions of many fairytales, particularly those collected and published in 1812 by the Brothers Grimm, the storybook wolves were far more sinister than their later, more child-friendly versions. In fact, in the original *Little Red Riding Hood* the wolf not only eats grandma, he finishes off Red Riding Hood as well! The first book of Brothers Grimm fairytales, called *Children's and Household Tales*, was often deemed unsuitable for children. It set off such an uproar that subsequent revisions have been toned down to reduce violence and suggestiveness. The story of *The Two Brothers* and their battle against a werewolf is probably the best known of the Grimm Brothers' lycan tales.

Penny Dreadfuls

The lycan in literature reached a high point in Victorian England in the mid- to late-1800s. At this time, especially with Alexandre Dumas's *The Wolf Leader* in 1857, supernatural approaches to the legends of the werewolf entered the popular imagination. In this tale, the vengeful anti-hero Thibault makes an agreement with the devil in the guise of a wolf who walks on its hind legs, and who wishes only to exploit Thibault's evil inclinations. Thibault gives the wolf a single hair from his own head for each person he wishes the wolf to harm. With the pact, Thibault is also granted the power to command the wolves in the forest. In Clarence Houseman's 1896 novel *The Werewolf,* the story centers around the unique concept that drops of blood from someone who's prepared to die for a loved one is a sufficient way to slay the demonic werewolf.

The popularity of the werewolf in the Victorian era was epitomized by works that were commonly referred to as *penny dreadfuls,* serialized tales printed on cheap paper a few pages at a time and sold for the price of one penny per section. Although the penny dreadful idea began in the 1830s as a way for respected authors to reach lower-class audiences, by the 1850s the penny dreadful market was flooded with sensational stories aimed directly at teenagers. Many of these tales included werewolfery in all its glory, the most famous being *Wagner the Werewolf.* In this story the aging hero, Fernand Wagner, is offered eternal youth, wealth, and good looks in exchange for serving the "devil," John Faust, for the last year of his life. The additional caveat is that Wagner is also turned into a werewolf. That's a pretty high price to pay for easy money and eternal partying, don't you think?

"Dracula's Guest"

Bram Stoker, author of the seminal 1896 vampire novel *Dracula,* dabbled in the lupine world when he wrote the short story "Dracula's Guest" in the late 1890s. The tale revolves around an unnamed German visitor to Transylvania who has an appointment with Count Dracula. The impetuous traveler ignores warnings to stay out of the forest and leaves his hotel room to wander among the trees. There he encounters the Countess Dolingen, a vampire, who conjures a blizzard before being struck by lightning and cast back into her crypt. During the snowstorm, the traveler is approached by a massive wolf with huge teeth who keeps the traveler warm and safe until help arrives. When rescuers come, they vainly fire on the wolf as it flees into the trees. Believing that it has harmed the traveler, they proclaim: "A wolf—and yet not a wolf . . . no use trying for him without the sacred bullet." Upon returning to his room, the traveler discovers a note from Dracula warning him: "There are often dangers from snow and wolves and night." Indeed, it was a warning that came too late to avoid a close encounter with a malicious vampire and a benevolent werewolf!

On the Prowl

DOTH THE MOON care for the barking of a dog?

—Robert Burton, British writer and clergyman

The Werewolf of Paris

While Bram Stoker's *Dracula* is generally considered to be the godfather of vampiric fiction, Guy Endore's 1933 novel *The Werewolf of Paris* became more of the odd uncle of lupine literature as the genre moved into mainstream fiction. In *The Werewolf of Paris*, the main character, Bertrand, is a child born on Christmas Eve—a forbidding sign for werewolfery—who later discovers that he's descended from a family of lycan heritage. Traumatized by increasingly disturbing nightmares and fantasies, Bertrand grows to young adulthood and heads to Paris to seek answers and peace. There he finds love with a beautiful tavern girl called Sophie, but his wolfish drives only increase. Fearing he'll harm Sophie, Bertrand flees into the city to act out his urges by hunting and feeding. Captured in his wolf form in the act of murdering a man in the sewers, Bertrand is sentenced to an asylum. Frustrated and bereft, he leaps to his death from the top of the building. Ironically, Sophie, who's unable to live without him, has also taken her own life. *The*

Werewolf of Paris is the seminal novel of permanent affliction, forbidden love, and tragedy. It became the basis for the 1961 film *The Curse of the Werewolf* with Oliver Reed, and the 1975 lycan romp *Legend of the Werewolf* starring Peter Cushing (see Chapter 11).

Running with the Pack

A crucial distinction made by experts in regard to early horror literature is that vampires, unlike werewolves, have had the huge literary advantage of building a genre based on Bram Stoker's seminal 1896 novel *Dracula* and Stoker's renowned precursors, including John Polidori's *The Vampyre: A Tale*, Thomas Malcolm Rhymer's penny dreadful *Varney the Vampire*, and Sheridan Le Fanu's novella *Carmilla*. By contrast, experts and historians note that the lycan realm is more an amalgam of myth and legend woven into early literature, some of which was introduced in novels such as *Dracula* and with Count Dracula's ability to shapeshift into a wolf. Now let's take a look at how this early lycan literature has evolved into modern-day werewolf fiction as seen through the eyes of some very ingenious writers.

Chapter 7

Full Moon Fiction

erewolf fiction in the modern age has taken shape across many genres, including science fiction, fantasy, horror, romance, and particularly in the young adult realm with series such as *Harry Potter* and the *Twilight* saga. What makes these books and their werewolves so much fun to read is that they all retain various aspects of mythology, real-life accounts, and especially lycan cinema. It's time for us to examine full moon fiction at its finest, and the authors who are brave enough to take on the exploration of man's inner beast.

Sci-Fi Shapeshifters

Werewolf fiction first made its way into the sci-fi book market in the 1950s, and it was directed straight at the newly burgeoning group of rabid science fiction fans. Such offerings as *Darker Than You Think* and *Wolves of Darkness* by Jack Williamson and "There Shall Be No Darkness" by James Blish were among the first sci-fi-oriented stories printed. One of the most fascinating aspects of werewolf fiction as a whole is that it generally defies specific description to any single genre, and covers a range of literary styles including sci-fi, horror, romance, adventure, and fantasy. Still, the sci-fi market of the mid-1900s helped introduce the werewolf legend to a brand new marketplace and left legions of fans howling for more.

On the Prowl

THE LIFE OF the wolf is the death of the lamb.

—John Clarke, American poet

Horrifying Hounds

The shivers of lycanthropic literature found yet another excited audience beginning in the 1970s and 1980s as popular fiction authors expanded wolf mythology into the horror genre. Among the first horror stories was Gary Brandner's 1977 novel *The Howling*, which begins when a middle-class woman named Karyn Beatty is attacked in her home by an unknown assailant and suffers a miscarriage. She and her husband, Roy, escape to the tiny town of Drago in the mountains of California, where a werewolf bites Roy in the forest. Much to her horror, Karyn soon discovers that the entire town is infested with homicidal werewolves, and she and a friend from the city, Chris, fight vainly to stave them off. Finally, Karyn and Chris inadvertently start a fire, which sweeps through town and into the forest, and the pair escape as angry howling fills the night air.

Full Moon Madness

Of course . . . everyone knows about werewolves.

—Evelyn Ankers as Gwen Conliffe in *The Wolf Man* (1941)

As you may have guessed, these new novels were often the basis for film adaptations, many of which bore only vague resemblances to their original stories. *The Howling*, for example, had six sequels after the 1981 original film. Still, the majority of the adapted books and the films did well in sales, and many continue to attract new generations of readers. Here are a few of the best in show:

- *The Howling* by Gary Brandner (1977), adapted for film in 1981
- *Wolfen* by Whitley Strieber (1978), adapted for film in 1981
- *Lost Prince* by Chelsea Quinn Yarbro (1983), originally released as *The Godforsaken*
- *Cycle of the Werewolf* by Stephen King (1983), adapted for film as *Silver Bullet*, aka *Stephen King's Silver Bullet*, in 1985
- *The Talisman* by Stephen King and Peter Straub (1984), adapted for television in 2009
- *The Dark Cry of the Moon* by Charles L. Grant (1986)
- *Howling Mad* by Peter David (1989)
- *Moon Dance* by S. P. Somtow (1989)

The Romantic Werewolf

Although vampires have been a staple of the romance genre for decades, many writers have recently discovered the allure of the werewolf, and some scribes, such as Laurell K. Hamilton with the *Anita Blake: Vampire Hunter* series, consistently delve into lycan mystique. A number of new writers eventually created stand-alone titles and entire series of books featuring the lives and losses of love-struck werewolves. Here are a few of those romantic undertakings:

- *Blood and Chocolate* by Annette Curtis Klause (adapted for film in 2007)
- The *Breeds* series by Lora Leigh
- The *Dark* series by Christine Feehan
- The *Dark Hunter* series by Sherrilyn Kenyon
- The *Hunter's Moon* series by Sherrie Scotch
- The *Killing Moon* series by Rebecca York
- The *Werewolf* series by Connie Flynn
- The *Wyndham* series by Mary Janice Davidson

Young Adults and Hairy Hooligans

When it comes to lycan literature, the young adult market has become a virtual gold mine for digging into new perspectives of the werewolf mystique. That began with the early efforts by C. S. Lewis in the 1951 magical romp *Prince Caspian*, which was the second book of the *Chronicles of Narnia* series. From those early beginnings grew the *Goosebumps* series that started in 1992, *Blood and Chocolate* by Annette Curtis Klause in 1999, and more recently Stephenie Meyer's *Twilight* saga. Since its earliest escape into the realm of young adult fiction, the clan of the werewolf has continued to overrun our imaginations. Here are a few favorites:

- *No Humans Involved* by Kelley Armstrong
- *Personal Demon* by Kelley Armstrong
- *The Wereling* series by Stephen Cole
- *The Icemark Chronicles* by Stuart Hill
- *The Wolving Time* by Patrick Jennings
- *Lonely Werewolf Girl* by Martin Millar
- *Death's Shadow* by Darren Shan
- *Red Rider's Hood* by Neal Shusterman

- *Tantalize* by Cynthia Leitich Smith
- *Lone Wolf* by Edo Van Belkom
- *Wolf Pack* by Edo Van Belkom

The *Twilight* Zone

Though primarily a young adult series that falls into the vampire genre, Stephenie Meyer's bestselling *Twilight* saga is a definite crossover into the lycan zone, a fact that will come to prominence with the release of future films that include her werewolf packs and pivotal werewolf character Jacob Black. The saga thus far includes *Twilight* (2005), *New Moon* (2006), *Eclipse* (2007), and *Breaking Dawn* (2008). As an added perk, the 2008 film adaptation, also called *Twilight*, has, as of this writing, raked in close to $380 million worldwide, surpassing *Van Helsing* as the top grossing vampire film of all time. Its sequel, *The Twilight Saga: New Moon*, is due to hit the silver screen in the fall of 2009 and will no doubt prove equally profitable. The majority of this literary and cinematic success is likely due to the teenage female contingent who are entranced by *Twilight's* forbidden love story between human and vampire and Meyer's depiction of the werewolf packs—the most prominent character being hunky Native American Jacob Black (see Chapter 2).

Forbidden Fruit

In *Twilight*, we are first introduced to Meyer's *la famille de vampires*, the Cullens, who are definitely *not* your typical blood-sucking family given that they are self-proclaimed vegetarians (meaning they subsist only on animal blood). The most eccentric of the Cullen brood is the irresistible and ethereally handsome Edward, who falls in love with tomboyish high schooler Bella Swan, a recent transplant from Arizona who now lives with her father (the town's sheriff) in the damp, dreary town of Forks, Washington. *Twilight* clearly focuses on Bella and Edward's relationship and the choices they both must make, all of which becomes a Pandora's box filled with supernatural forbidden love. And once the box is opened—which it is—there's no turning back.

On the Prowl

WITH SO MANY vampires encamped in the neighborhood, a werewolf population explosion was inevitable.

—**Stephenie Meyer, American author**

In Meyer's second installment, *New Moon*, Edward breaks up with Bella and the entire Cullen family moves to Alaska to preserve Bella's safety, at which point her relationship with werewolf Jacob Black comes to the fore. Though despondent and still pining for her bloodsucking boyfriend, Bella is able to guess that Jacob is a werewolf. In Meyer's tales, while the lycan gene is present in the Quileute males (with the exception of Leah Clearwater, the lone female werewolf), it only becomes active when a vampire is nearby. In Jacob's case, the proximity of the Cullen family is enough to trigger his ability to transform into a werewolf.

The werewolf pack in *New Moon* must bond to protect Bella against the evil Victoria, whose vampire lover, James, was killed by the Cullens at the end of *Twilight*. We learn through this revenge match that, while Jacob and his kind are voluntary werewolves and can transform at will, he often transforms merely by becoming angry. Another twist is that the Quileute werewolves don't chronologically age once the shapeshifting takes effect. Jacob is actually sixteen but looks to be twenty-five. As with most lycans, Jacob and his kind possess heightened senses, superhuman strength and agility, and also the unique trait of having an elevated body temperature. They don't turn into snarling hellbeasts, just larger-than-life versions of wolves normally seen in the wild. Meyer also explains early on that Jacob's great-grandfather made a treaty with the Cullens, promising that the werewolves wouldn't attack them as long as they didn't kill or bite any humans and agreed to stay off Quileute land.

Amid her depression at the loss of Edward, Bella becomes a daredevil, riding motorcycles and cliff diving, during which she almost dies. Jacob saves her before she drowns, but Edward, believing Bella to be dead, ventures to Italy to seek the help of the governing vampires called the Volturi for the sole purpose of wanting to die. At *New Moon's* end, Bella finds Edward before he achieves his suicidal plan, but the Volturi insist that because she knows the secret of the vampires, she must become a vampire herself or die. In a family vote, much to Edward's dismay, the Cullens determine that Bella will be turned after she graduates. Through it all, there's no doubt that Jacob is developing strong feelings for Bella, and he is indeed angry when the Cullens return to Forks.

Fighting the Dead and the Undead

In *Eclipse*, the third installment of the *Twilight* series, which is told from Jacob's perspective, Meyer accelerates the teen angst and forbidden love subtext, which this time centers around the Cullens' uneasy alliance with the werewolf class, as they unite to fight Victoria and an army of newborn vampires she's created to avenge James's death. In another subplot, Edward asks Bella to marry him, a fact Jacob learns as the three of them are sequestered during the battle. After Jacob threatens to intentionally lose his life during the fight, Bella realizes that she loves him. She seals her resolve with a kiss—leaving her to choose between her vampire boyfriend and an irresistibly handsome werewolf. Of course, after Edward kills Victoria and the battle is won, Bella tells Jacob that she's decided to marry Edward and that she too will become a vampire. This news causes Jacob to transform into a werewolf and disappear into the woods.

In *Breaking Dawn*, Meyer deviates from her standard format, telling the story in a trio of separate parts. The first part, as told by Bella, focuses on the wedding and honeymoon, during which they learn that she is pregnant with Edward's "child." Part 2 is told from Jacob's point of view as Bella, given the hybrid species she's carrying, experiences an insanely fast and dangerous gestation period. Complicating the plot is the fact that the werewolf pack want to kill the child, believing it will do harm to humans. Jacob refuses to accept the plan and leaves the pack to form his own, attracting the loyalty of female werewolf Leah Clearwater and her younger brother Seth. When giving birth, Bella, nears death and is turned into a vampire by Edward. But in order to turn her, Edward needs Jacob's blessing so as not to break the vampire/werewolf treaty. Despite Jacob's initial dislike—and the feelings of the other werewolves—upon seeing the infant girl Renesmee, he immediately "imprints" on her. She is his soul mate and, under werewolf law, is forever kept safe from harm by the pack.

Part 3 of *Breaking Dawn* is again told from Bella's point of view, focusing on her newfound vampirism and a battle with the Volturi. The Volturi mistakenly assume that Renesmee began life as a human child who was turned into a vampire—a strict no-no under vampire law—instead of being born a cross-bred creature of a human and a vampire. The Cullens end up winning the battle when Renesmee shows her special power of sharing memories to the Volturi.

Meyer's fifth installment of the saga, *Midnight Sun*, was leaked on the Internet, causing her to halt the writing process. What is certain is that *New Moon* is arriving at a theater near you in 2009, and will likely break records across the all-time list in both the vampire and lycan categories.

The Lycanthropic Professor Lupin

It should come as no surprise to anyone that we find werewolves within the magical world of British author J. K. Rowling's *Harry Potter* series. The primary werewolf is Professor Remus Lupin, his first name no doubt playing on the mythical Roman tale of Remus and Romulus (see Chapter 1), and his last name being another word for werewolf. His first appearance in the series is in Rowling's third installment, *Harry Potter and the Prisoner of Azkaban*, in which he's the professor of the Defense Against the Dark Arts at Hogwarts School of Witchcraft and Wizardry. He later appears in *Harry Potter and the Order of the Phoenix* and *Harry Potter and the Half-Blood Prince* before he is killed in *Harry Potter and the Deathly Hallows*. Bitten by werewolf Fenrir Greyback as a child, Lupin has had a lifelong fight with lycanthropy, and he suffers further public scorn when Hogwarts Potions Master Severus Snape publicly exposes Lupin as a werewolf.

Nicknamed "Moony" as a young student at Hogwarts, Lupin had, for the most part, been able to quell his inner beast courtesy of Hogwarts headmaster Albus Dumbledore. Dumbledore created the Shrieking Shack, where Lupin could retreat during the nights of the full moon. Later, at the behest of Dumbledore, Snape created a secret wolfsbane potion that Lupin could take monthly to prevent his full moon madness. But in *Prisoner of Azkaban* we finally see the full snarling werewolf come to light, when Lupin is caught without his potion during a full moon and enters into a fight with Sirius Black in Black's Animagus form of a black dog.

Though Lupin plays a part in the novels, particularly in *Prisoner of Azkaban*, it's his transformation in the film adaptation that truly brings him to life as a werewolf. Played by David Thewlis, Lupin undergoes a stunning metamorphosis from man to drooling bipedal werewolf in a CGI (Computer Graphics Imaging) feast for the eyes. Kept intentionally dark, the battle between Lupin and Sirius is a frightening display of just how quickly a man's inner beast can completely consume both his body and mind.

Moon Men

From Gilgamesh to Jacob Black to Remus Lupin, the literary lycan genre has not disappointed and likely never will in the decades to come. Now, it's time to turn your attention to the true center of the werewolf mystique, the hundreds of amazing werewolves who've appeared right before your very eyes on the silver screen. From *The Wolf Man* to *Underworld: Rise of the Lycans*, it's time to grab your leash and prepare to meet the best and boldest canines in cinematic history, starting with the genesis of silver screen werewolves.

Chapter 8

The Genesis of Werewolf Cinema

After exploring werewolves in the literary realm, it's only natural that we take a look into the true core of werewolves as we know them today. Cinematic lupines of the modern era are quickly becoming the crème de la crème of horror consumption, with their glowing eyes, drippy fangs, and hair sprouting in places from which hair just shouldn't sprout! It must be said that myth, legend, and literature aside, the majority of what we know—or *think* we know—about werewolves comes as a result of film. And so we begin with the birth of lycan cinema and how its legendary roots have grown to lunatic proportions.

What Makes a Great Celluloid Lupine?

The frightening form of the werewolf didn't make an appearance on the silver screen until the little known 1913 silent film *The Werewolf.* However, most experts cite the 1935 Universal classic *Werewolf of London* as the first "official" werewolf film. Since then, folks have maintained a healthy if not fanatical interest in the evolution of cinematic lycans—the more hair and danger the better. The most intriguing part of werewolf cinema is how it came to fruition, and that for more than eight decades, filmmakers, writers, cinematographers, technicians, computer graphics specialists, and especially special effects makeup artists have continually and brilliantly pushed the boundaries of transforming ordinary human actors into werewolves—the likes of which we could only begin to conjure up in our dreams.

Building a Better *Wolf Man*

Lycan lore, as you learned in Chapter 1, dates back to the ancient Egyptians and Greeks and has progressed over the centuries through European and American legends, superstition, and real-life accounts (see Chapter 2). But unlike vampires who have a symbiotic relationship with their history, the werewolf in film bears only a distant resemblance to the lycans of myth, legend, and literature. For that reason, much of what the general public associates with werewolves comes from the fertile imaginations of filmmakers, with only vague and sometimes entirely invented versions of actual legends.

It's important to understand just how unique werewolf cinema is, in that it was born as a result of a series of occurrences that combined to become the baseline for our understanding of werewolves to the present day. The first effort was a treatment, or narrative outline, called *The Wolf Man* written by Robert Florey in 1931. Then came the 1935 film *Werewolf of London*, followed by Curt Siodmak's scripts for the 1941 film *The Wolf Man* and one of its sequels, *Frankenstein Meets the Wolf Man*, both of which starred Lon Chaney

Jr. These four cinematic undertakings are the grandfathers of cinematic lycanthropy.

To Bark or *Not* to Bark . . .

During the Golden Age of horror in the 1930s and 1940s, we were treated to a host of what have become the definitive classic movie monsters including Boris Karloff as the Monster in *Frankenstein* (1931), Im-Ho-Tep in *The Mummy* (1932), Bela Lugosi as *Dracula* (1931), and Claude Rains as *The Invisible Man* (1933) to name a few. With the initial success of those films, each of the characters spawned many sequels, knockoffs, and parodies that crossed the horror genre line into drama, adventure, science fiction, and comedy. What was missing from the movie monster madness was the werewolf, and studio execs were more than excited to build the perfect *Wolf Man.*

Full Moon Madness

Harold Howard (played by James Hampton): For one thing, you're going to be able to do a lot of things the other guys aren't.

Scott Howard (played by Michael J. Fox): Oh yeah? Like chase cars and bite the mailman?

—Werewolf Harold Howard talking to his son, Scott, the morning after Scott's first werewolf transformation in *Teen Wolf* (1985)

In 1931, the original *Wolf Man* treatment was penned by French writer and film director Robert Florey, who at the time was directing *Murders in the Rue Morgue* starring Bela Lugosi. Florey's treatment was subsequently sold to Universal as a project meant for Boris Karloff. The idea was carefully discussed, but it was eventually abandoned by Universal in the early 1930s because the story was deemed too extreme for the general public. In his original storyline, Florey focuses on a young Bavarian boy named Christoph who is raised by the wolves that killed his family. Interestingly, Florey's choice of the name *Christoph* may have been based on Saint Christopher, who was thought to be half-man, half-dog in early Eastern European Christian legends (see Chapter 2). Florey also plays on the Roman myth of Remus and Romulus and their upbringing by a pack of wolves (see Chapter 1).

According to some experts, Florey's original treatment had Christoph suckled by a female wolf who happens to be a werewolf, which in turn causes the boy to become a lycan. Highlighted in the story is one of Christoph's human-to-wolf transformations, which takes place inside a confessional booth. This religious connotation contributed to the shelving of the film, given that the studio feared reactions of the Catholic church and other religious groups. It's said, however, that bits and pieces of Florey's original storyline made it into several Universal horror films, one of which is director Stuart Walker's 1935 offering *Werewolf of London*.

Getting in the "Loup"

As the first real lycan flick, the 1935 film *Werewolf of London* is like most of Universal's pictures of the era in that it's slick, it's well orchestrated, and it set several precedents for all future werewolf flicks. What kept it from being heralded as the preeminent werewolf film—which the 1941 *Wolf Man* would achieve—is the werewolf character himself, a respected botanist named Dr. Wilfred Glendon. Played by Henry Hull, Dr. Glendon isn't the sympathetic man-beast character that audiences could get behind. That disconnect exists partly because the storyline suffers from a strong dose of *Jekyll and Hyde* and *Invisible Man* influences that left Glendon more of a secretive high-society mad scientist than a mentally and physically tortured werewolf. Regardless, the film is important to werewolf evolution.

FULL BLOOM MADNESS

Werewolf of London begins with an expedition in the Himalayas, as Dr. Glendon searches for a rare and elusive flower called the *mariphasa lupino lumino* (the phosphorescent wolf flower), a strange bloom that grows only in Tibet and is said to take its life from the light of the moon. As fate would have it, just as Glendon finds his specimen, he's attacked and bitten by a werewolf, who we soon learn is the alter-ego of Dr. Yogami, a professor at the University of Carpathia, played by Warner Oland of *Charlie Chan* fame.

After Glendon's return to England, he becomes utterly obsessed with forcing the mariphasa to bloom, especially after Yogami shows up and explains the flower's ability to halt lycanthropic transformation. Yogami asks for a clipping of the flower, and telling Glendon that: "The werewolf is neither man nor wolf, but a satanic creature with the worst qualities of both." He also ominously warns Glendon, "The werewolf instinctively seeks to kill the thing it loves best." This rather foreboding statement holds true for many werewolf films throughout the decades. Later that night, we're shown Glendon reading a passage from a book that further explains the plight of the werewolf. That passage reads:

> *Transvection from man to werewolf occurs between the hours of nine and ten at the full of the moon, the essence of the mariphasa blossom squeezed into the wrist through the thumb at the base of the stem is the only preventive known to man. Unless this rare flower is used the werewolf must kill at least one human being each night of the full moon or become permanently afflicted.*

BY THE LIGHT OF THE MOON

After a series of murders has occurred, Dr. Yogami visits Scotland Yard. He relates to detectives that the mariphasa is the only known antidote for werewolfery, that there are two lycans on the loose, and that the flower is the only thing that can keep a werewolf from transforming. He also explains to the skeptical authorities that unless they secure the mariphasa plant and "discover the secret of nurturing it in this country, there'll be an epidemic that will turn London into a shambles."

Full Moon Madness

Remember this, Dr. Glendon: The werewolf instinctively seeks to kill the thing it loves best.

—Warner Oland as Dr. Yogami in *Werewolf of London* (1935)

The first time we're given a glimpse of Glendon's transformation is when he's able to force the mariphasa to bloom under a manufactured moonlight lamp. At that moment, Glendon's hand begins sprouting hair and he realizes that what Dr. Yogami has said to him is true. For the era, Henry Hull's on-screen transformation is relatively well executed and, although most viewers consider Lon Chaney Jr.'s transformation in *The Wolf Man* as the first authentic on-screen change, it bears noting that the *Werewolf of London* transformations were done by renowned makeup artist Jack Pierce, who did the makeup for both films. Pierce was also the makeup artist for such horror classics as *Dracula*, *Frankenstein*, *Bride of Frankenstein*, and *The Mummy*, among many other classics of the era.

Cleverly filmed, as most werewolf flicks are, and given that CGI (Computer Graphics Imaging) and the incredible makeup tricks of today didn't even exist, *Werewolf of London* manages to get the ball rolling for all future werewolf films. The film set a precedent for, among other things, werewolf transformation during the full moon, blooming plants, and the clear half-human half-wolf form that werewolves take on. Glendon's transformation occurs as he walks past a trio of pillars and a large bush in his garden. Each pillar he passes shows more of his lycan mutation, including his fangs, pointed ears, hands, and hairy facial features. His basic human shape, however, remains intact, which places him in the "mostly human" werewolf classification (see Chapter 4). What is apparent, given that time between the theatrical release of *Werewolf of London* and *The Wolf Man*, is that Jack Pierce took a different approach when making up Lon Chaney Jr.'s lunatic lupine. Hull's hairy demeanor appears much more slicked back and less wolflike than Chaney's, which experts often attribute to the fact that filmmakers and, more likely, studio execs didn't want to overly shock and frighten audiences. They wanted viewers to be able to recognize Henry Hull as the werewolf, whereas with Chaney they truly wanted an unrecognizable and scary man-beast.

Lacking the appeal of other Universal classics of the thirties, *Werewolf of London* wasn't a commercial success. Six years would pass before Universal would take another stab at bringing a werewolf to light, and it was up to director George Waggner and writer Curt Siodmak to make sure the lycan bit the big screen with fantastic fortitude.

The Wolf Man's "Destiny"

By 1941, German screenwriter, filmmaker, and novelist Curt Siodmak rewrote Robert Florey's *Wolf Man* treatment from scratch, changing the title to *Destiny*. Before the end of filming, in a move likely meant to make the film more marketable, the name was changed to *The Wolf Man*. To ensure its success, Universal hired a stellar cast, including Claude Rains, Ralph Bellamy, Bela Lugosi, Evelyn Ankers, Patric Knowles, Lon Chaney Jr., and Maria Ouspenskaya. Filmed in only three weeks in the winter of 1940, *The Wolf Man*—which played as a double-feature alongside *The Mad Doctor of Market Street*—became a huge hit. Within several months, the film grossed a million dollars, which for the era was definitely considered a commercial success. But let's start from the beginning.

In the earlier drafts of the script, the lead character, Lawrence Talbot, was named Larry Gill, and instead of being an English lord and son of Sir John Talbot, he was an American engineer dispatched to Talbot Castle to install a telescope. In the final film, of course, Larry Talbot *is* Sir John's son, who returns from California after eighteen years and the death of his older brother to assume management of the family estate.

Siodmak was reportedly quite displeased with the casting of Lon Chaney Jr., given that the Oklahoma-born Chaney bore absolutely no resemblance to an English lord in accent or behavior.

The plot of *The Wolf Man* is quite simple; its underlying themes, however, are far more complex. Once Larry Talbot arrives at his father's mansion he meets Gwen Conliffe, daughter of a local antiques dealer, and purchases a cane that has a silver handle in the shape of a wolf head with a pentagram etched on it. That evening, Larry accompanies Gwen and her friend Jenny into the misty woods in order to have their fortunes told by a traveling gypsy Bela (Lugosi), who is under the watchful eye of his mother, Maleva (Ouspenskaya).

Lugosi, who has only seven lines in the film, reads Jenny's fortune only to visualize a pentagram on her palm. At that point, it becomes clear that Bela is a werewolf. He tells Jenny to leave, but she's quickly and ferociously attacked by a four-legged wolf (Bela) as she runs through the dark woods. Larry comes to her aid, but during the struggle the wolf bites him, thus beginning his lycanthropic curse. He does manage to kill the beast, but by the time help arrives the wolf has reverted to Bela's human shape. What follows is the slow progression of how Larry comes to grips with the fact that he believes himself to be a werewolf and the fact that no one, aside from Maleva, believes him no matter how frenzied his actions become. By the end of the film, it is Sir John (Rains) who beats the werewolf to death with Larry's silver cane, only to recoil in horror as he and Maleva witness Larry, whose leg is caught in a bear trap, transform from a werewolf back into human form. One of the curious and amusing issues about the film that experts continue to debate is the fact that Bela turns into a four-legged wolf, as you would see in the wild, while Larry is a bipedal werewolf who maintains the majority of his human form (see Chapter 4). After all these years, no one can figure out why that happens! Even more interesting is that one of the most prized props—Larry's silver-tipped wolf head cane—used in *Wolf Man* still exists today. As luck would have it, renowned horror and sci-fi memorabilia collector Bob Burns was friends with the son of Ellis Burman—a prop maker and special effects technician of the era—who created the cane. After filming, the silver wolf head handle, which was allegedly made of vulcanized rubber, was given by Burman to Burns, who cherishes it to this day.

LUPINE REALITY OR FANTASY?

What makes *The Wolf Man* crucial to werewolf cinema is its multileveled subtext, which includes isolation from society, public scorn, depression, good versus evil, religion, possible schizophrenia, and a very strong effort to make Larry Talbot's transformation intentionally vague. The viewer is meant to wonder whether Larry actually shapeshifted or if it was all in his mind. The film begins, in fact, with a book passage citing the definition of lycanthropy:

> *LYCANTHROPY: (Werewolfism). A disease of the mind in which human beings imagine they are wolf-men. According to an old LEGEND which persists in certain localities, the victims actually assume the physical characteristics of the animal. There is a small village near TALBOT CASTLE which still claims to have had gruesome experience with this supernatural creature. The sign of the Werewolf is a five-pointed star, a pentagram . . .*

It's said that Siodmak's original script included scenes of Larry seeing himself in his werewolf form in a mirror or a puddle, thus adding to the wonderment of the lycanthropy being all in his mind. But in the end studio execs cut most of those psychological elements out of the film, a tactic that film critics have constantly debated, citing that the film may have had more depth had those scenes remained. The vague aspect of psychological impairment that remains in *The Wolf Man* is reinforced by Sir John when he explains to Larry a type of schizophrenia, the scientific definition of which is the very simple Greek definition of "The good and evil in every man's soul. In this case, evil takes the shape of an animal." Sir John furthers his point by mentioning that he believes that "most anything can happen to a man in his own mind." This is reinforced at several points throughout the film. After being bitten by Bela, there is no sign of a wound on Larry's chest, which pays homage to the werewolf of legend and his ability to regenerate. In another scene, Larry sees a pentagram on his chest—something that *isn't* visible when he later shows it to Sir John. Though in the film's final cut this psychological aspect is downplayed, it does still leave viewers wondering if in fact Lawrence Talbot is imagining all of his lupine suffering. Of course that theory doesn't really explain the attacks we see Larry commit, but it is one aspect among many conceived by Siodmak that is retained, and noticeably accelerated, in the four *Wolf Man* sequels that continue to follow Larry Talbot's travails.

Full Moon Madness

Is this what you want? I've lived by their rules my entire life. I've protected them, envied them, and for what? To be treated like an animal? We are NOT animals! We *do* have a choice. We can choose to be more than this. We can be slaves . . . or we can be LYCANS!

—Michael Sheen as Lucian, addressing the enslaved werewolves in *Underworld: Rise of the Lycans* (2009)

Another aspect of *The Wolf Man* that experts and historians continue to debate is the almost surreal setting of the film. As experts and historians often mention, the town and castle are implied to be set in Wales, but Wales is never mentioned. This is likely due to studio execs worrying about offending the Welsh, given Sir John's mention at one point in the film that "we are a backward people." The time frame is also impossible to ascertain given the village's mix of motorcars, horse-drawn wagons, gypsies, and Americans mixed in with British aristocrats. Part of that surreal undertone and the varied subtexts have a great deal to do with Curt Siodmak's personal background.

Siodmak, who became a permanent fixture in the cinematic horror world, began his career in his native Germany. It's said that he and his film director brother Robert fled to England in 1933 after hearing an anti-Semitic speech by Reich Minister of Propaganda Joseph Goebbels, which signaled that Nazi power was just beginning its stranglehold on Germany. With that experience embedded in Siodmak's psyche, *The Wolf Man* maintains a strong anti-Nazi undertone that Siodmak himself acknowledged in a 1999 article, saying, "I was forced into a fate I didn't want: To be a Jew in Germany. I would not have chosen that as my fate. The swastika represents the moon. When the moon comes up, the man doesn't want to murder, but he knows he cannot escape it, the *Wolf Man* destiny." It's also said that Siodmak's script for the 1940 film *The Invisible Man Returns* is heavily influenced by his frightening past as a man who was forced to flee his own birthplace.

Although it was cutting-edge technology for the time, the somewhat dated appearance of the special effects used in the film doesn't diminish *The Wolf Man's* power, and the story cannot be underestimated when it comes to modern-day werewolf perception. The most popular and memorable aspect of the film is a very simple four-line poem that's repeated several times in the first few minutes of the film, and which is very often credited as a verse that originated in werewolf mythology. Not so. Siodmak invented the verse for *The Wolf Man* and it has since become the iconic prayer of the werewolf:

Even a man who is pure in heart
And says his prayers by night
May become a wolf when the wolfsbane blooms
And the autumn moon is bright.

A Predestined End

In discussing *The Wolf Man* one would be woefully remiss to not mention the actress who many critics and experts cite as one of the shining stars of the film. That star is Maria Ouspenskaya who, as Maleva the gypsy woman, *is* the spiritual and supernatural conscience of the story. She also gives the film a strong measure of Greek tragedy and Eastern European gypsy superstition that has made its way into many werewolf films. A two-time Oscar nominee and renowned acting coach in both her native Russia and Hollywood, Ouspenskaya was the perfect choice for Maleva, the only person who believes and truly understands what Larry is going through, and who famously recites her "predestined end" verse after both Larry and Bela meet their fate. A main character in *Wolf Man's* 1943 sequel *Frankenstein Meets the Wolf Man*, Maleva flat out tells Larry that she considers him her "son," and when he insists on finding a way to die, she goes to great lengths to take him to Frankenstein's Castle in the hopes that the good doctor can cure Larry's lycanthropy. Not the greatest plan, but as you'll now learn, it makes for outstanding classic horror!

Frankenstein Meets the Wolf Man

Universal's *Frankenstein Meets the Wolf Man* plays a strong role in the cinematic evolution of the werewolf on several levels, not the least of which is Larry Talbot's massive acceleration in *both* his human and werewolf behavior. Directed by Roy William Neill with a screenplay written by Curt Siodmak, this outing gives us a significantly more goal driven Larry, whose overriding wish throughout the film is to die and finally be rid of his wretched curse.

Taking its cue from Hammer Films and the successful use of resurrection in their classic vampire films, Universal decided to employ the same tactic. In Chapter 5, you learned that wolfsbane is an age-old werewolf repellant. In *Frankenstein Meets the Wolf Man*, Siodmak takes full advantage of that fact in resurrecting Larry Talbot from his coffin. Set four years after Larry's demise in *The Wolf Man*, a pair of grave robbers break into the Talbot family crypt hoping to swipe any jewelry or other valuables that Larry was buried with. Upon opening his coffin, they discover that Larry hasn't aged a day since his "death." They also notice that his body is covered with dried flowers—which one fellow realizes is wolfsbane. Regardless, his buddy foolishly removes the plants in order to pilfer Larry's ring. As the full moon shines brightly through the crypt and onto Larry's body, he immediately awakens and mutates into the Wolf Man. Naturally, he kills one of the thieves and is eventually found in the village unconscious in his human form. Despite ending up in a hospital, and having brain surgery and subsequent amnesia, Larry's lycanthropy becomes stronger, indeed rivaling his need to kill himself to be rid of the curse. At that point, he tracks down Maleva (Ouspenskaya) and together they travel to the village where Frankenstein's Castle is located in the hope that Dr. Frankenstein can cure Larry's werewolfery. No such luck. The castle stands in ruins under guard by suspicious villagers who are still traumatized by the rampage of the evil Frankenstein Monster and his maker—both of whom they proudly slayed.

On the Prowl

WE OFTEN SEE men changed into wolves at the turn of the moon.

—Gervase of Tilbury, thirteenth-century British religious cleric

Larry and Maleva become hunted targets of the villagers after Larry releases Frankenstein's Monster (Bela Lugosi) from his icy grave in the vague hope of finding Dr. Frankenstein's diary and the secret to life and death. They do find the diary, with the help of the late doctor's daughter, Baroness Elsa Frankenstein (Ilona Massey). Also in the picture is Larry's surgeon, Dr. Frank Mannering, played by actor Patric Knowles who portrays Gwen Conliffe's fiancée, Frank

Andrews, in *The Wolf Man*. As one would expect, Mannering goes a bit mad with power in his experimentation and, as Larry and the monster are undergoing another epic electrical treatment, a rebellious villager blows up a dam and destroys the castle—thwarting their plan. The ending is left intentionally ambiguous, and we don't know for certain if Frankenstein or Larry manage to escape the destruction. A fun bit of trivia is that one of the prominent villagers who is out to slay the Wolf Man is played by Dwight Frye, who in 1931 became legendary for his role in director Tod Browning's *Dracula*, starring Bela Lugosi and Frye as his demented servant Renfield. This time around, Frye has his full faculties and is out to destroy the wolfish invader.

What's different in this installment of the *Wolf Man* saga is that Larry's desperation and frantic wish to die is exceptionally dire. Part of that is due to the rabid scorn and societal pressure that permeates the film's subtext. Not just one monster is ostracized—but two, which makes for double trouble. Also enhanced is Chaney's physical transformation from man to wolf. Done once again by makeup artist Jack Pierce, the transition is much more seamless and arguably more effective than the 1941 film (see Chapter 10). In *Frankenstein Meets the Wolf Man*, the moon is also a primary feature. Unlike its predecessor, there are plenty of moon shots and everything Larry does is dictated by the lunar cycle.

Like *Wolf Man*, this second installment contains much of the same subtext including good versus evil, isolationism, regeneration, panic, and rejection by proper society. The ambiguous psychological impairment, however, isn't quite as prominent as the original film, which is likely due to the fact that Siodmak was more comfortable with Larry's character as he appeared in the final cut of *Wolf Man*. Ultimately, what makes *Frankenstein Meets the Wolf Man* so important is that it furthers Larry's progression as a werewolf, especially his utter desperation and increased temper. In that regard, this first sequel does well to set up the tortured plight of the Wolf Man as it continues in *House of Dracula* and *House of Frankenstein*.

The Bane of Our Existence

The concept of lycan transformation during the full moon, as well as the use of blooming wolfsbane and silver as a means of destruction, is almost always attributed to *The Wolf Man* writer Curt Siodmak. Few, however, mention that *Werewolf of London*—a film released six years prior to *The Wolf Man*—clearly shows its werewolf transformations during the full moon. There are literally *no* shots of the moon in *The Wolf Man* or mention of a full moon other than the famous *Wolf Man* verse. Transformations and attacks by both Bela and Larry are triggered by a pentagram appearing in the palm of their next victim, and *not* by the moon. In *Frankenstein Meets the Wolfman*, that issue is resolved with a host of moon shots initiating Larry's mutations. There's also the correlation between the mariphasa flower and its blooming to the blooming wolfsbane picked by Jenny and tossed away by Bela in *The Wolf Man* and its further mention in the verse. Though it's rarely discussed, both of these issues beg the question of who truly devised the concept. It's even possible that some of these crucial aspects were derived from Robert Florey's original treatment.

The idea of using silver bullets as a way to kill lycans could very likely have come from earlier references as well. In 1812, a story called *The Two Brothers* appeared in the first collection of fairytales written by the Brothers Grimm. At the time, the book was called *Children's and Household Tales,* which later became the legendary *Grimm's Fairytales.* In that particular tale, one of the brothers uses silver buttons from his jacket as bullets to shoot a witch (see Chapters 5 and 6). Silver was also used as a deterrent in Bram Stoker's 1896 novel *Dracula,* when Van Helsing used a silver crucifix when he and his cohorts invaded Dracula's lair at Carfax Abbey. This means that laying claim to various aspects of werewolfery can be tenuous at best given the sheer number of myths, legends, and literary works that make reference to various ways of defeating the dark side.

Howling Good Times

Though fascinating and complex in its birth, the cinematic werewolf has a strong base on which to stand. This will become even more evident in the next chapter, when we focus on the best werewolf films to date. Each of the highlighted films is important in the continuing evolution of the big-screen howler, and no doubt there will be many more to come in the future. One thing, however, is certain—whenever the moon is full, you'd be wise to turn the other direction if a sudden howl pierces the silence of the night!

Legendary
Cinematic Lupines

A s with any film genre, there are scores of B-movies included in the mix. But amid all those cheesy half-baked plots and bad special effects, there are more than a few stellar celluloid gems that leave enthusiastic audiences clapping and begging for more. With well over 300 films dedicated to werewolves, there are plenty of fan favorites from which to choose. In this chapter, the best in show are highlighted for you in all their lycanthropic glory.

Fire in the Blood

There is little dispute among experts and historians that legendary characters such as the Wolf Man, Frankenstein, Dracula, the Mummy, the Invisible Man, the Creature from the Black Lagoon, and dozens more monsters have helped build the horror genre. There's also little debate that the filmmakers who first brought these critters to the big screen set in stone the idea that, as a cultural medium, movie monsters have the ability to blatantly and subliminally reflect what is occurring in society during various eras. As noted, the 1941 film *The Wolf Man* and its follow-up, 1943's *Frankenstein Meets the Wolf Man*, have a subtext of World War II and anti-Nazi undertones. Likewise, a trio of films released in 1981 have a chilling subtext, but this time it was wholly inspired by a much different yet equally deadly real-life tragedy that found its way into the werewolf genre. Though it was already a major concern prior to 1981, it wasn't until that year that the Centers for Disease Control declared AIDS an official pandemic. The fact that cinematic lycanthropy is primarily passed on by a werewolf bite or scratch that effectively poisons an individual's blood makes the AIDS issue a blatant underlying theme.

Also playing into that issue is the societal fallout of the disease, including isolationism, public scorn, anger, and extreme terror of contracting AIDS or, for that matter, any sexually transmitted disease. Each of the three werewolf flicks released in 1981, *The Howling, Wolfen,* and *An American Werewolf in London*, are very different in their approach and storyline, but ultimately the message is the same: As a civilization, we need to take care of our own no matter what the situation. It also must be said that it's no small coincidence that the number of werewolf films doubled in the 1980s and 1990s to more than fifty films per decade, and the 2000s have seen more than seventy films thus far.

The Howling

Say what you will about the 1981 film *The Howling*, but after more than two decades, the film is still scary and humorous and holds firm at number nine on Box Office Mojo's all-time top-grossing werewolf flicks. Loosely based on the 1977 novel by Gary Brandner, the original had so much potential that it was enough to give birth to a franchise of six sequels from 1985 to 1995. Directed by Joe Dante, *The Howling* begins with the capture and destruction of serial killer Eddie Quist (Robert Picardo), who happens to be a werewolf (see Chapter 10). But its primary focus is on female news anchor Karen White (Dee Wallace of *E.T.: The Extra-Terrestrial* fame), who helps catch Quist. On the advice of psychiatrist Dr. Waggner (Patrick Macnee), White then retreats to Waggner's recuperative center, which turns out to be a colony of werewolves not unlike the leper colonies in ancient history. Once White's husband is turned into a voracious werewolf by a resident she-beast, all hell breaks loose and the real fun begins.

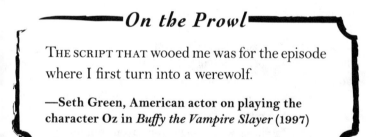

On the Prowl

THE SCRIPT THAT wooed me was for the episode where I first turn into a werewolf.

—Seth Green, American actor on playing the character Oz in *Buffy the Vampire Slayer* (1997)

Loaded with a cast of heavyweights, including Wallace, Macnee, Kevin McCarthy, John Carradine, Slim Pickens, and Kenneth Tobey, *The Howling* has a lot going for it in regard to werewolfery that at times also crosses over into witchcraft all wrapped around a few tidy plot twists, including the fact that Quist is alive and well, that Dr. Waggner is promoting a mainstream book called *The Gift*, and that at his colony, Dr. Waggner is actually attempting to keep the werewolves on an animal, not human, diet! Like many lycan films, *The Howling* makes use of the full moon, and silver bullets as a means of destroying werewolves.

One bit of cool trivia is that Joe Dante and *Howling* writers John Sayles and Terence Winkless paid homage to the directors of classic lycan films by naming many of the film's characters after them, including George Waggner (*The Wolf Man*), R. William Neill (*Frankenstein Meets the Wolf Man*), Erle Kenton (*House of Frankenstein* and *House of Dracula*), Terry aka Terence Fisher (*The Curse of the Werewolf*), Lew Landers (*The Return of the Vampire*), Jerry Warren (*Face of the Screaming Werewolf*), Sam Newfield (*The Mad Monster*), and Fred aka Freddie Fisher (*Legend of the Werewolf*). It's a nice touch, among many, that Dante employs amid the dark humor of *Howling*, which breaks new ground with the help of Oscar-winning special effects makeup artist Rick Baker and Rob Bottin. To be certain, Eddie Quist's transformation earns him a place in the cinematic lycan Hall of Fame (see Chapter 10).

Wolfen

Director Michael Wadleigh's film *Wolfen* approaches lycanthropy from a much different angle than the majority of werewolf cinema. The story is based on the 1978 novel by Whitley Strieber who, in 1983, wrote the vampire cult classic *The Hunger* and the controversial 1986 alien abduction tale *Communion*. *Wolfen* deals with lycanthropy from a more spiritual and cerebral angle by bringing in Native American werewolf lore. In this case, the Native American werewolves are called *wolfen*, and they've cohabitated undetected with humans for over 20,000 years. Oscar-nominated actor Albert Finney stars as retired New York City detective Dewey Wilson, who's called upon to solve a series of grisly attacks that appear animalistic in their execution. Along with a rather cheerful coroner, played by Gregory Hines in his second major film role, Dewey enters a supernatural world that appears to defy reasonable explanation.

The brutal murders include, among others, the grisly deaths of an influential land developer and several homeless people, and they lead Dewey and his partner to an abandoned church in an area of the city that is being demolished for development.

The investigation eventually leads to a young, seriously intense Native American activist named Eddie Holt (Edward James Olmos). Interestingly, this is one of the few films where we see no human-to-wolf transformations. Instead, *Wolfen* treats the werewolves as a separate but superior species who have roamed the area for years and survived by killing only the unwanted derelicts of human society. The werewolves come to light only *after* developers encroach on their hunting grounds in the slums and force the werewolves into the open.

Wolfen's strong Native American slant is something that isn't highlighted in Strieber's novel, so not only does the finished film reflect endangerment of the human species as well as the animals, it also addresses the issue of Native American history among civilized man. Another of the unique aspects of *Wolfen* is director Wadleigh's use of shots from the wolf's point of view, almost as if we're seeing the wolf's stalking through night vision goggles. It's a very effective tactic that lends itself well to the story's supernatural element. At the film's end, when Dewey is surrounded by the wolf pack, his understanding of the wolfen and the respect he's paid to them ultimately saves his and his partner's lives and sends the wolfen back into hiding.

An American Werewolf in London

Released a few months after *The Howling* and *Wolfen*, *An American Werewolf in London* is an alternately serious and humorous roller coaster ride that flat out addresses the plight of a normal guy who becomes ravaged by lycanthropy to a disastrous end. Starring David Naughton, Griffin Dunne, and Jenny Agutter, the film focuses on two buddies, David Kessler (Naughton) and Jack Goodman (Dunne), who are backpacking through the English countryside when they're attacked by a werewolf. Jack dies and David wakes up in a hospital attended to by Alex Price (Agutter), with whom he forms an instant relationship.

By all accounts, the film's storyline follows the typical werewolf evolution of realizing that you're becoming a werewolf, recognizing that you're attacking innocent folks, and eventually deciding on your inevitable disappearance or demise. What sets *American Werewolf* apart from the majority of lycan flicks is writer and director John Landis's perfect frenzied melding of horror and humor. Add to that the bizarre fact that throughout the film, David is visited by and converses with his dead friend Jack, who with each appearance becomes more and more decomposed. David's relationship with Jack and with Alex comes full circle by the film's end, when at one point he tells an extremely decrepit Jack that "a werewolf can only be killed by someone who loves them." In this case, it is indeed Alex who bears witness to David's demise as he's trapped at the end of an alley and shot by the authorities.

Full Moon Madness

Carl (played by David Wenham): According to the book, you won't turn into a werewolf until the rising of your first full moon. That's two nights from now. Even then, you'll still be able to fight Dracula's hold over you until the final stroke of midnight.

Van Helsing (played by Hugh Jackman): Sounds like I have nothing to worry about.

Carl: Oh my God . . . you should be terrified!

—From *Van Helsing* (2004)

In truth, the premiere of the film marked a turning point in the history of cinematic lycanthropy. As *The Howling's* Eddie Quist began the new age of modern on-screen werewolf transformation, so too did Naughton's spectacular transformation, something that we see in all its full bodily glory with amazing realism, courtesy of the talents of Rick Baker, who also did the special effects makeup for *The Howling* and won an Oscar for his

work on *American Werewolf.* Despite David Kessler's sad end due
to a gunshot, it's Baker's talents that help keep David Naughton's
performance firmly in the werewolf Hall of Fame (see Chapter
10), and the film ranked at number six on Box Office Mojo's all-
time werewolf list, earning more than $30 million to date.

The *Underworld* Trilogy

There's much to be said about the brilliant and commercially
successful *Underworld* trilogy in all its vampiric and lycanthropic glory. Not only are the vampires sleek and hip, but the
lycans are—bar none—the best cinematic werewolves ever
seen. Created by a host of talented artists, technicians, stunt
professionals, CGI wizards, and actors, the lycan transitions to
enormous, muscular, snarling, bipedal werewolves are incredibly seamless, and so fluid in their movements and convincing
in their expressions that they're utterly mesmerizing.

What sets the tone for the entire trilogy is a blood war
that's been fought for close to a thousand years between vampires and the werewolves who once served as their daylight
guardians. In the first installment, *Underworld*, we're introduced to Lucian, the most feared leader of the lycan clans, who
in all three films is perfectly portrayed by Welsh actor Michael
Sheen (see Chapter 10).

Underworld is primarily focused on vampire "death dealer"
Selene (Kate Beckinsale), Lucian (Sheen), vampire coven leader
Kraven (Shane Brolly), vampire elder Viktor (Bill Nighy), and
Michael Corvin (Scott Speedman), the unfortunate human descendent of the omnipotent Alexander Corvinus, from whose
sons all vampires and lycans are descended. The latter characters serve as the storyline for *Underworld: Evolution*, which
picks up where the first film ends, while the third installment,
Underworld: Rise of the Lycans, belongs entirely to Lucian, a
prequel that drives home the very essence of his complex and
heroic werewolf character.

In *Underworld*, you get a real sense of the werewolf plight.
As the vampire covens live a life of wealth in the security of a
lush mansion, Lucian and his lycan clan are a rather unkempt

bunch forced into hiding and residing deep underground in tunnels below the subway system. As with many genre films, the *Underworld* trilogy runs a strong subtext that focuses on the differences between the upper and lower classes, social outcasts, lethal viruses, reformation, revenge, redemption, evolution of the species, forbidden love, and the ultimate supernatural battle between good and evil.

Like many of the traditional werewolves, Lucian's pack has an aversion to silver—but with a twist. If managed in time, they can remove silver bullets when shot and quickly regenerate. But they can't survive the liquid silver nitrate the vampires develop, which directly enters the bloodstream. Sadly, it's Lucian who learns that one the hard way.

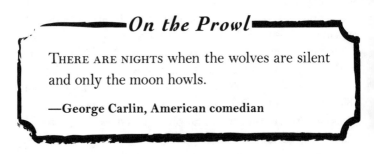

On the Prowl

THERE ARE NIGHTS when the wolves are silent and only the moon howls.

—**George Carlin, American comedian**

It's worthy to note that the trilogy has the distinction of being the only set of films that crosses the line in terms of box office gross by being on the top ten all-time list for both vampire and werewolf films, with *Underworld: Evolution* raking in more than $111 million worldwide, *Underworld* more than $95 million, and *Rise of the Lycans* more than $87 million since its January 2009 release.

Brotherhood of the Wolf

It's a good guess that most directors wouldn't venture to make a historical period film based on a werewolf, but director Christophe Gans's 2001 film *Le Pacte des Loups*, also known as *Brotherhood of the Wolf*, pays off in spades. Easily one of the best films of the genre, *Brotherhood* follows the true-life tale of the infamous Beast of Gévaudan, the notorious and particularly vicious lycan who plagued Southern France from 1764 to 1767 (see Chapter 2). As with all historical adaptations, the film obviously takes plenty of creative licenses for the purpose of its plot, but in this instance those changes are highly effective.

The king's royal botanist, Grégoire de Fronsac (Samuel Le Bihan), is sent by King Louis XV to Gévaudan after several murders. He is accompanied by his faithful and lethal companion, Mani, a Native American Iroquois stunningly played by Mark Dacascos, himself an accomplished martial artist. After studying one of the beast's victims, Fronsac ascertains that their foe is over 500 pounds, which effectively rules out all of the previously slain wolves as being the murderous culprit. Added into the mix is Fronsac's love interest, Marianne de Morangias (Émilie Dequenne); her sibling-obsessed brother, Jean-François de Morangias (Vincent Cassel); priest Henri Sardis (Jean-François Stévenin); and a mysterious Italian prostitute named Sylvia (Monica Bellucci), who turns out to be far more than the average brothel babe.

What results in this frantic and historic werewolf chase is a labyrinth of intrigue, deception, intense romance, murders, a secret society, gypsies, Vatican espionage, underground religious zealots, astonishing action sequences, and one *seriously* scary werewolf. Whew! Who knew you could pack that much into a historically based lycan flick? What makes *Brotherhood* so incredibly engaging are the first-rate performances by Le Bihan and Dacascos and the tension and surprising plot twists that, like the wolf itself, lurk amid the shadows of a dense forest, waiting to strike. If you're a true fan of lycan cinema, you absolutely don't want to miss *Brotherhood of the Wolf.*

Dog Soldiers

Another of the best lycan films is a 2002 independent British production replete with a fabulous cast, slick werewolves, major plot twists, and a whole lot of no-holds-barred fast action that keeps you firmly planted on the edge of your seat. Written and directed by Neil Marshall, *Dog Soldiers* focuses on a group of young infantry soldiers dropped in the middle of the forested Scottish Highlands for a routine training mission. Of course, it doesn't take long to figure out that this is no ordinary mission. What makes *Dog Soldiers* so good, aside from the fact that its intensity never slows down, is that there is not one but three very different werewolves, all of whom are worthy of the lycan Hall of Fame (see Chapter 10).

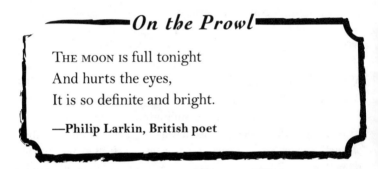

On the Prowl

THE MOON IS full tonight
And hurts the eyes,
It is so definite and bright.

—**Philip Larkin, British poet**

Led by Sergeant Harry Wells, who's exceptionally well played by Sean Pertwee, and Kevin McKidd as standout soldier Private Cooper, the team quickly realizes that something is afoot in the dense forest when they rendezvous with a special ops team that's been brutally wiped out save for their barely alive and totally ruthless commander, Captain Ryan (Liam Cunningham). What ensues is what appears to be a losing battle with enormous, incredibly agile, vicious werewolves, who begin eliminating the soldiers in a frenzied attack, during which Wells is literally gutted but still alive.

At that point, out of nowhere, a zoologist named Megan (Emma Cleasby) drives past and rescues what's left of the team, taking them back to an isolated farmhouse owned by a local family. With both Ryan and Wells wounded, Cooper comes to the fore, barricading everyone in the house for a hellish night fighting a pack of werewolves that are *literally* beating at the doors and windows.

Not long after their arrival at the farmhouse, it becomes evident that Ryan's mortal wounds have healed, which in the werewolf world can mean only one thing. Cantankerous and secretive of the true purpose of his mission, which was in fact to capture one of the werewolves, Ryan is the first of the insiders to transform and join the lycan pack. Polar opposite of the evil Ryan is Wells, who realizes his fate given how fast *his* wounds are healing. And then there's Megan herself, who we come to find out is actually part of the werewolf family and who eventually lets the pack inside the house. After a truly explosive ending, there are only two survivors—the resourceful Private Cooper and the family dog.

The *Ginger Snaps* Trilogy

If there was an award for the most eccentric lycan film it would unanimously go to the *Ginger Snaps* trilogy released in 2000 and 2004. An independent Canadian production, the original film focuses on the lycanthropic travails of two teenage sisters living in suburbia with their June Cleaver-esque mom (Mimi Rogers) and a dad who's clearly overwhelmed by estrogen. Both Emily Perkins and Katharine Isabelle, who respectively play Brigitte and Ginger Fitzgerald, are beyond stellar, and they are further detailed in the lycan Hall of Fame in Chapter 10.

Ginger Snaps

The upshot of the first installment, *Ginger Snaps*, is exactly that—Ginger does indeed "snap" in a big way when she's bitten by a werewolf. What ensues is utter mayhem as this pair of goth-oriented sisters attempt to deal with the fact that Ginger, having the added stress of getting her first period, begins a conversion from boy-hater to insatiable seductress. Of course, it doesn't help that she's sprouting a tail, some mean fingernails, and a seriously rabid canine disposition. Younger sis Brigitte takes a different tact and works toward finding a cure, only to eventually set in motion both of the sisters' damnation.

Ginger Snaps: Unleashed

The second film, *Ginger Snaps: Unleashed* is Brigitte's story. In an effort to honor their pact to be "together forever," Brigitte intentionally infected herself with Ginger's lycan blood in *Ginger Snaps*. Now she must stave off her own inevitable doom, which she attempts by injecting herself with liquid monkshood to squelch her growing beast within. At the same time, she has to deal with her ghostly big sis dishing out advice, and also run away from yet another snarling mutated mauler (see Chapter 4) who wants to mate with her. Suffice it to say, throughout the story poor dear Brigitte *never* has a good hair day.

Ginger Snaps Back: The Beginning

Ginger Snaps Back: The Beginning is a daring move on the part of filmmakers as it takes place not in the present day, but in the Canadian wilderness in 1815. In this offering, the sisters are holed up with a small group of soldiers in a remote fortress with a pack of werewolves (called *wendigos*) surrounding the place. What's interesting about the timeline of the third installment is that it lends itself to the fact that if reincarnation does indeed exist, these unfortunate siblings are doomed to relive the same fate over and over for eternity. Fortunately for cinematic lycan fans, these flicks are a blast . . . so bring it on!

Teen Wolf

Whether it's adventure, drama, or comedy, there's no denying the charisma of Michael J. Fox, and in 1985 he outdid himself in what's become an enduring cult classic for the werewolf genre. Ranked sixth on Box Office Mojo's all-time list of top grossing lycan films, the comedic *Teen Wolf* is the ultimate coming of age—or shall we say coming of wolf—story, which feeds off a tumultuous combination of teen angst, puberty, and lycanthropy. Scott Howard (Fox) is the typical high school wallflower: He's infatuated with the super-hot popular girl who ignores him, and he ignores the ordinary girl next door who loves him. What doesn't help is that his angst is brought out by his seriously bad basketball team, which is on a major losing streak.

Scott's first physical transformations fall in line with the story's pubescent subtext as he begins to notice strange things happening to his body during a party. By the time he gets home, he's sprouted hair most teens grow only in their worst nightmares. That night he learns that his family has a dark secret: His dear old dad is also a werewolf and has passed the affliction on to his son. How's that for bad genetics? Of course, as any normal teenager would do when handed a curse, he finds a way to use it to get the girl. For Scott, this means revealing his big bad incredibly hairy self to everyone and working his magic on the basketball court, and even surfing atop a speeding van. The moral of the story? Be careful what you wish for, because having to out yourself as a teen wolf and becoming a sideshow attraction isn't the easiest way to get a date for the prom!

Van Helsing

Hugh Jackman's unlikely turn as a werewolf in the 2004 blockbuster horror extravaganza *Van Helsing* brilliantly showcases an amalgam of reluctant and voluntary werewolves that are rarely seen on the big screen (see Chapter 10). Once bitten, Van Helsing (Jackman) embraces his fateful condition for the sole purpose of killing his immortal foe, Count Vladislaus Dracula (Richard Roxburgh). Jackman's lycan is a massive, muscular hulk of jet-black hair, whose entirely wolfen face can quickly revert from a bloodthirsty werewolf when he attacks Dracula to an incredibly sympathetic character when he realizes that he's accidentally killed his lady love, gypsy princess Anna Valerious (Kate Beckinsale). At that precise moment, werewolf cinema is graced with one of its more memorable and spectacular shots: the werewolf Van Helsing holding the limp Anna in his arms, a bright full moon showcasing his silhouette as he howls in pain. That howl is extended and masterfully transformed from lycan to human as Van Helsing's coarse animal hair literally melts from his body. His height and human form return to normal, but that painful howl continues to pierce the night. It's a beautifully structured scene that truly epitomizes the plight of the traditional werewolf: They always hurt the ones they love the most.

Full Moon Madness

Why does it smell like wet dog in here?

—David Wenham as Carl in *Van Helsing* (2004)

The lycan transformation of Anna's brother, Velkan Valarious, is even more stunning and belies the intense horror of the situation. A young, strong, and handsome man who's spent his life attempting to kill Dracula, Velkan is ultimately made to do Dracula's bidding and is sent to slay Anna and Van Helsing. In human form Velkan is terrified, angry, and entirely sympathetic. His condition is anything but voluntary. In fact, at the film's opening it's Velkan himself who attempts to trap and kill one of Dracula's werewolf slaves, which makes Velkan's curse all the more ironic.

Once converted, Velkan is the consummate reluctant werewolf. In a rather painful and frantic transformation, he quickly begins a series of violent movements, as if he is having a seizure, and during those movements he tears at his clothing and his skin, which rapidly dissolves from his body to reveal a completely hairy, fierce, and enormous werewolf. His reversion back to human form is equally mesmerizing. Velkan's metamorphoses, like Van Helsing's, are well accomplished on the part of Kemp, Jackman, and the CGI technicians and special effects artists.

There are several things that set these two werewolves apart from the garden-variety howler. The first is the action of ripping off their skin, which is one aspect drawn from mythology whereby suspected werewolves were sometimes cut in order to ascertain if fur appeared under their skin (see Chapters 4 and 10). In addition, both Van Helsing and Velkan have the unique distinction of actually flipping back and forth from werewolf to human if clouds happen to pass over the moon when they are in their lycan or human form. The third aspect is that, while Velkan sadly dies in the film, Van Helsing is actually cured by being injected with a serum that Dracula guards for the sole purpose of returning any werewolf he suspects is capable of killing him to human form. As far as on-screen werewolves go, Jackman and Kemp are two of the best, so if you're a werewolf fan you'll most definitely want to indulge in *Van Helsing*.

Blood and Chocolate

Ranked fourteenth on Box Office Mojo's list of all-time werewolf films is director Katja von Garnier's 2007 film *Blood and Chocolate*. This film, which is based on the novel by Annette Curtis Klause, is worthy of note primarily for its portrayal of true wolf pack dynamics, for the Romeo and Juliet subtext, and for its gorgeous human-to-wolf transformations.

The forbidden romance in this film begins when teen lycan Vivian (Agnes Bruckner)—sulking in a church in the middle of the night—meets Aidan (Hugh Dancy), a graphic novel artist who's in Bucharest, Romania, studying and drawing loup-garou, as they're referred to throughout the film. As luck would have it, Aidan looks upon lycanthropy as transcendence, and he believes loup-garou are blessed rather than cursed. Clueless to the fact that Vivian is part of a pack, he innocently pursues her, much to the chagrin of her fellow pack members and their leader, Gabriel (Olivier Martinez), who's soon to name Vivian as his next mate.

Aside from its quirky title, which obviously equates blood as a symbol of the lycanthropic disease, and chocolate indicating the chocolaterie in which Vivian works, this film is unique in its telling on several accounts. For starters, it shows werewolves as a family, with a hierarchy based on wolves in the wild. The leader is strong and bold, the women are extremely maternal and nurturing, and the young werewolves are seemingly obedient. It also reveals a strong heritage, as it focuses on lycan history and that this pack and their kin have existed for more than 5,000 years. Though they've been driven out of most major European cities, they remain safe and undetected in Bucharest, and indeed, make earnest attempts to blend into normal human society.

Like most cinematic lupines, this pack can also can be destroyed by means of silver weaponry and be burned, which harkens back to werewolf mythology and legend where individuals believed to be lycans were burned at the stake (see Chapter 2). Aidan himself eliminates Gabriel's son by touching his neck with a silver necklace, and he also—during his frenzied and clever escape during an official werewolf "hunt"—kills several of the pack with a silver dinner knife!

More than anything, the most intriguing and beautiful thing about this pack of hounds involves their transformation. Instead of becoming snarling, drooling bipedal beasts, their change is a simplistic metamorphosis from human to wolf. When they jump, their human form is completely engulfed in bright glowing light, and you can just make out their silhouette changing from elongated human to canine while in the air. By the time they hit the ground, they are completely transformed wolves, each a different color and size so as to be distinguishable. Some experts suggest this type of transformation is likely due to an effort to keep the film's budget low, but it does prove effective, especially in scenes when the entire pack is gathered for their full moon "hunt" for a deviant human of Gabriel's choosing. In that regard, *Blood and Chocolate* offers yet another unique twist to the genre. These monthly hunts, though ritualistic in their isolated forest setting, show members of the pack meeting as a human family while also working together as a werewolf family to capture their human prey. Ultimately, *Blood and Chocolate* boils down to the quintessential Shakespearean tragedy of forbidden love, but in this spin on the *Romeo and Juliet* tale, love *does* conquer all.

Wolf

Paying no mind to the critics' split assessments regarding director Mike Nichols's 1994 film *Wolf*, this werewolf foray remains, as of this writing, the highest grossing werewolf film to date. According to Box Office Mojo, *Wolf* has collected just over $65 million domestically and another $66 million internationally for a total worldwide gross of almost $132 million, which bests the number two rated film, *Underworld: Evolution*, by more than $20 million.

With *Wolf*, there appears to be no gray area in regard to its appeal: Folks either love it or hate it. Regardless of that fact, one thing is for certain—Mike Nichols loaded his film with heavyweights, including Jack Nicholson, Michelle Pfeiffer, Christopher Plummer, James Spader, David Hyde Pierce, and Kate Nelligan. *Wolf*, in many ways, mirrors the dog-eat-dog (literally, in this case) world of high-end publishing. In this werewolf romp, the ruthless Raymond Alden (Plummer) has taken over a publishing company that employs senior editor Will Randall (Nicholson) and Randall's protégé and head of marketing, Stewart Swinton (Spader). Pfeiffer plays Alden's terse and troubled daughter, Laura, with Nelligan portraying Randall's wife, Charlotte.

From the moment Randall is bitten by a wolf on a snowy back road, his life begins to change in ways that at first seem to be for the better. He acquires the typical werewolf perks of heightened senses, energy, strength, prowess, and even more important, cunning when it comes to dealing with Alden after Alden demotes him from his long-held position. And not only is Randall losing his job, but his two-faced protégé, Stewart, has pulled a fast one in order to move up the food chain—he gets Randall's job and is bedding his wife. Contrary to his normal roles, Nicholson is actually playing a nice, moral guy, but given his newfound werewolf confidence—despite its confusion and addiction—he's willing to play the game and fight to keep his job.

What sets *Wolf* apart from other werewolf flicks is that it picks up elements of the traditional Lon Chaney Jr. lycan while it also approaches the affliction with a restrained combination of zeal, deep spirituality, and goodness of the soul that Randall knows deep down will somehow prevail. This subtext is reinforced when Randall seeks the advice of a professor who tells him that the wolf does give in to consumption, save for his nature and his heart. Through it all, you get the sense that Randall—no matter his actions—is staying the course and doing the right thing, be it outwitting Alden and Stewart to get his job back, taking up with Laura, or even handcuffing himself to a hotel radiator so as not to harm anyone. In the end, Randall *is* a normal guy coming to terms with the beast within.

Minions of the Moon

So now that you've had a taste of some of the best werewolf films in horror history, let's truly indulge *your* inner beast by reading all about the werewolves who comprise the lupine Hall of Fame. As you've likely surmised, there are more than a few werewolves roaming the cinematic forest, and each one has put a new spin on the consummate lycan.

Chapter 10

Hall of Fame Howlers!

*I*n the last chapter we explored the best that werewolf cinema has to offer and a range of films that explore the depth of man's ability to remain calm amid a lycanthropic storm. And let's face it, becoming, combating, or curing a werewolf in all his or her hairy glory is no easy feat. Now let's do the howlers due diligence by honoring the actors and actresses whose bark *and* bite have earned them a spot in the coveted cinematic lycan Hall of Fame.

Lon Chaney Jr.

If you ask people who their favorite movie werewolf is, most typically cite Lon Chaney Jr. as having firmly left his paw prints on horror history. And while *The Wolf Man's* Lawrence Talbot has indeed become a seminal character of the genre—one often mentioned in the golden triad of movie monsters along with Dracula and Frankenstein's Monster—he's by no means the only hound dog who's suffered the curse of lycanthropy or left bite marks on unwilling victims, whether it be in the horror, sci-fi, history, or comedy genres.

To give you some idea what Lon Chaney Jr. had to professionally overcome, consider that his actor father Lon Chaney Sr.—known in the film industry as "The Man of a Thousand Faces"—had in a mere seventeen years beginning in 1913 more than 150 acting roles to his credit. Chaney Sr. left an indelible mark on movie history as both an actor and consummate makeup genius. His son, however hard he tried, would never quite attain that stature, a fact that would, in many ways, continue to haunt him.

Born Creighton Tull Chaney in 1906 in Oklahoma, Chaney Jr. eventually followed in his father's footsteps, but it wasn't until 1935 that marketing efforts to capitalize on his father's fame forced the hulking actor to change his screen name to Lon Chaney Jr. and in many of his films, simply Lon Chaney. His first big break came in 1939 with the coveted role of Lennie Small, the mentally challenged Depression Era migrant worker in director Lewis Milestone's Oscar-nominated film *Of Mice and Men.* Chaney took immense pride in portraying Lennie and held that and his role as Larry Talbot above all others. In 1942, he played the monster in *The Ghost of Frankenstein* and also the mummy, Kharis, in *The Mummy's Tomb.* A year later, he donned a cape to take his turn as Count Alucard (a palindrome for *Dracula*) in *Dracula's Son.* But it was his 1941 portrayal of Lawrence Talbot in director George Waggner's *The Wolf Man* that would forever cement Chaney's place in lycan horror history.

In Chapter 8 you read about the evolution of *The Wolf Man,* but what hasn't yet been mentioned is Chaney's actual makeup transformation, which has been written and speculated about for decades. Renowned makeup artist Jack Pierce is the mastermind behind Chaney's werewolf good looks in both *The Wolf Man* and the 1943 sequel, *Frankenstein Meets the Wolf Man*, and it was a task that took endless grueling hours of applying makeup and adhering appliances to Chaney's head, arms, and legs. For the era, actors like Chaney who submitted to such transformation shots would lay their head in some type of headrest to stay still. In this case, speed graphic cameras and portrait cameras with frosted glass—that literally had Chaney's outline drawn onto the glass—were triangulated so as to keep the image steady and focused on Chaney. He was then photographed, and presented in a series of images called *lap dissolves* in order to show his transformation. It may not seem scary today given the current use of CGI, but at the time it proved frightening to gaping audiences. Oddly enough, the only time we see Chaney's face fully transform is *after* Larry Talbot's killed and returns to human form.

The first transformation we're shown focuses only on Larry's shins and feet, upon which he wore custom-made boots cast to form wolf's paws that enabled Chaney to walk on the balls of his feet. During the rest of the film, we only see Chaney in his fully finished lycan persona. In the original Robert Florey treatment, the Wolf Man is only seen in reflections such as in puddles, but in Chaney's *Wolf Man*, it isn't until forty-two minutes into the film that we actually get to see Larry Talbot as a fully transformed werewolf attacking the gravedigger who's digging what one assumes is the grave of Bela Lugosi's last victim.

If you get the chance to watch *The Wolf Man* on DVD, there's a terrific running commentary by film historian Tom Weaver, in which he tells all kinds of great facts about the actors, the making of the film, and especially the makeup process which experts have been debating for decades. One thing Weaver relates from his sources is that makeup artist Jack Pierce likely started by giving Chaney a prosthetic nose stuffed with cotton and collodian, followed by the application of grease paint and powdering. Weaver, like some historians, surmises that Pierce would likely have had a number of ventilated hair pieces created, made of yak hair that was laced and crocheted onto silk or nylon netting. The next phase of transformation is still argued by experts and historians, though many surmise that Pierce carefully applied spirit gum to Chaney's face, cut the hair at various angles and placed it on his face, and finally singed it with a curling iron to make the ends more rough. The final touch is thought to be a wig that was secured to cover Chaney's eyebrows and pulled clear down to the nape of his neck. Molds were also said to be made of made of the front and back of Chaney's hands to create slip-on gloves, and fangs allegedly made of ivory, wood, or hard dental wax were also created.

In the 1943 sequel *Frankenstein Meets the Wolf Man*, the makeup and photography process was taken one step further. This time, technicians created a plaster pillow complete with wrinkles glued in place and an indentation for Chaney's head. This kept his head steady, and as makeup was applied made for a much more fluid photographic transition into the Wolf Man. Despite all attempts to ascertain how long it took to apply Chaney's makeup and film the dissolves, no one knows for certain given that the documentation for *Wolf Man* no longer exists. The subject, however, remains a hot topic among experts and historians.

When it comes right down to it, Chaney and his alter ego Larry Talbot set the standard for all future lycans. Larry was the ultimate reluctant werewolf, afflicted with werewolf melancholy, confusion, frenzy, social ostracism, and an aversion to silver—all of which is countered by a sympathetic demeanor. It's safe to say that Chaney truly *is* the granddaddy of the cinematic werewolf genre. He played Larry Talbot in five films, including *Wolf Man*, *Frankenstein Meets the Wolf Man*, *House of Frankenstein*, *House of Dracula*, and *Abbott and Costello Meet Frankenstein*. He also appeared as a werewolf in the 1962 *Route 66* episode *Lizard's Leg and Owlet's Wing*, and the 1960 Mexican film *La casa del terror* aka *House of Terror*. But when speaking of Larry Talbot, Chaney often said that: "The Wolf Man was mine—all alone."

Michael Sheen

As a vampire film, the *Underworld* trilogy is first-rate. As a lycan film, it's even better. That fact is due to Welsh actor Michael Sheen, who in all three films hauntingly and brilliantly portrays Lucian, the most powerful leader of all the lycan clans. As mentioned in Chapter 9, we're first introduced to Lucian, an ancient lycan whose clan members have the ability to transform into werewolves at will, in *Underworld*. The vampire covens, believing him slain centuries earlier, are unaware that he's plotting revenge against evil vampire elder Viktor (Bill Nighy) and is searching for the last remaining descendent of his bloodline so as to combine vampire and lycan blood to form a new species. The poor soul doomed to that fate is Michael Corvin (Scott Speedman), who's in a tug of war between Lucian and defiant vampire Selene (Kate Beckinsale).

Through flashbacks in *Underworld* that are entirely played out in *Underworld: Rise of the Lycans*, we come to find out that Lucian's true motivation for slaying Viktor is Viktor's cold-blooded killing of his vampire daughter Sonja, who was Lucian's lover and pregnant with his child. Given that loss, Lucian's quest to turn Michael into a new species—one that is stronger than both vampire and lycan—becomes an obsession that comes to fruition just as Lucian perishes at the end of *Underworld*.

Though Sheen's performance in *Underworld* is superb, it's in *Rise of the Lycans* that Lucian's full story comes front and center and where Sheen truly shines. Indeed, at times Sheen makes Lucian appear almost biblical in his expression and determination to break free of not only his physical enslavement by the vampires, but also of the complex mental enslavement of his inner beast. In *Rise*, a prequel to the original, we finally get to see and understand the labyrinth of Lucian's long life, and how his infectious blood made him the bearer of a strain of voluntary werewolves who could transform at will. We also see and feel his anger as he's enslaved by Viktor, while engaged in a love affair with Sonja (Rhona Mitra). The final battle for supremacy is epic, spurned on by the dark, menacing medieval setting and a single werewolf whose sheer will, intelligence,

THE GIRL'S GUIDE TO *Werewolves*

and capacity for love enable him to embrace for the better what most werewolves consider an incredible curse.

Of all the silver screen lycans that we've seen to date, Lucian is hands-down the most engaging on all psychological levels and across all transformative capacities. He's also unique in regard to his bloodline (having descended from werewolves who could not revert to human form), his attitude, and the fact that he doesn't fall into the classic werewolf "type" of being a voluntary or involuntary lycan (see Chapter 4). Though he possesses qualities of both, he is far more complex in his intellect and physicality and how he uses both to his best advantage. Lucian is, quite simply, the best lycanthropy has to offer.

Full Moon Madness

Lucian (played by Michael Sheen): Were you not afraid of them?

Raze (played by Kevin Grevioux): Yes, but I wanted to live.

Lucian: Are you afraid of me?

Raze: Yes.

Lucian: Well do not be. I will not bite . . . much.

—Lucian to Raze after an encounter with the bloodthirsty horde of werewolves created by William Corvinus in *Underworld: Rise of the Lycans* (2009)

In a surprising turn of events, Michael Sheen will now be switching sides from werewolf to bloodsucker. It was recently announced that after assertively pursuing the award-winning actor, Sheen has accepted the role of Volturi vampire leader, Aro, in the highly anticipated *The Twilight Saga: New*

Moon. Like horror legends Boris Karloff, Bela Lugosi, and Lon Chaney, it will be fascinating to see how Sheen will cross the genre and transfer his carefully honed dark side sensibilities from one cursed monster to another.

David Naughton

Most likely you don't remember the famous Dr. Pepper commercials of the late 1970s and early 1980s, which featured a catchy "I'm a Pepper; you're a Pepper" jingle. The star of one of those commercials was none other than David Naughton, who as a result of that exposure was cast to play lycanthrope David Kessler in John Landis's 1981 landmark film *An American Werewolf in London.* And with that film, we were at last given a glimpse into the spectacular and painful process of shapeshifting.

Full Moon Madness

I'm afraid, sir, that I gave up my belief in goblins, witches, personal devils and werewolves at the age of six.

—Henry Hull as Dr. Glendon in *Werewolf of London* (1935)

When David Kessler transforms it comes on in an instant. He burns with fever and quickly strips off his clothes. As he watches in horror, his right hand begins to elongate to that of an exaggerated wolf's paw, after which we see him drop on all fours to expose the fur on his back, his feet stretching, and hair sprouting all over his body. It's so well done that you truly feel his utter torment—you hear the bones crunching, hair sprouting, and his spine and muscles popping out. Fangs, claws and facial features then begin contorting as the final spectacular transformation shows his ears and snout growing and extending, along with a flash of his golden eyes, before the scene dissolves to a shot of the full moon. It truly is a thing of beauty.

As far as the horror genre is concerned, David Kessler's transformation has to rank among the top ten best scenes of all time, if for no other reason than it set the bar for all werewolf films to follow. It's also exceptionally seamless, and totally cool. There's no question that the Oscar that special effects makeup artist Rick Baker received for *American Werewolf* is well deserved. But aside from Baker's groundbreaking effects, Naughton must also be credited for his portrayal, because in truth, his charming and sympathetic demeanor make him one of the most likeable silver screen lycans in horror history.

War Wolves

Neil Marshall's 2002 film *Dog Soldiers* is easily one of the best werewolf films of the genre, and that is in no small part to Sean Pertwee, Liam Cunningham, and Emma Cleasby, who give us three very different and very memorable cinematic lupines (see Chapter 9). While *Dog Soldiers* is tightly woven, its major asset consists of its two main lycans, Sergeant Harry Wells (Pertwee) and Captain Ryan (Cunningham), who fall into two distinct types of werewolf. Ryan revels in the power and embraces the gift without question while Wells, realizing his fate, becomes the rebellious lycan determined to wipe out the entire invading pack—himself included.

Having soldiers barricaded in a remote farmhouse with a pack of enormous and seriously vicious werewolves surrounding the place is the perfect setup for internal chaos, and *Dog Soldiers* in that respect is a winner. Both Ryan and Wells are near death when they're rescued in the woods. After a few hours, Ryan's wounds have healed but his arrogance hasn't, a fact that dominates his transformation directly in front of the bewildered soldiers, including Wells, who realizes that only hours before he was also on death's door. By the film's end, when Wells can no longer hold off the transformation, he secures the only other survivor, Private Cooper, in the basement and lures the family of lycans into a gas-filled kitchen, setting everyone alight in a blaze of glory. Cunningham and especially Pertwee are both exceptional in their roles, and in a genre where it's easy to look like a cheesy, overly stuffed Yeti, these two lycan Hall of Famers are anything but.

Robert Picardo

If there's one scene-stealer in the 1981 wolf-fest *The Howling*, it's the now-legendary transformation of killer werewolf Eddie Quist, played by Robert Picardo. Given that *Howling's* premiere predated *An American Werewolf in London* by a scant few months, it was Picardo we first saw transformed on the big screen, and as a result, cinematic werewolf morphology was changed forever.

For the transformation of Eddie Quist, special effects make-up artists Rick Baker and Rob Bottin took full advantage of new special effects, particularly air bladders under the skin, to allow for muscle and limb elongations and implosions, fang extensions, and the ultimate in facial mutation. You literally hear bones cracking, fingers elongating into claws, Eddie's chest and limbs expanding, ears emerging from his head, and hair sprouting in a slow but incredibly seamless change from human to snarling hellbeast. As far as lycan transformation goes—you don't want to miss the metamorphosis of Eddie Quist.

Michael J. Fox

In the 1985 comedy *Teen Wolf,* Michael J. Fox brings a ridiculously cute twist to the werewolf persona as Scott Howard, the teenage protégé of a long line of lycans with a "slight" genetic flaw. In a tale of puberty taking a rather unusual turn, Scott, in his newly embraced werewolf form ignores the girl next door in favor of the insufferable popular girl. He's also part of the truly awful high school basketball team who get trounced in virtually every game they play. As a coming of wolf story, *Teen Wolf* can't be beat in that it truly does blatantly equate puberty, teen angst, and social pressure with lycanthropy. Scott's initial transformation is utterly hysterical and well done—if not totally over the top. He's by far the hairiest werewolf ever to hit the big screen! But watching the sheer horror of that first morphing brings into focus just how much angst teens suffer. Even funnier is that once Scott has transformed inside a locked bathroom, his father demands that he open the door, and when he does the poor kid is astonished to see that his own dad is also a full-blown werewolf who sheepishly utters the priceless line: "An explanation is probably long overdue."

As one might guess, Scott goes on to become the star of the basketball team by playing virtually single-handedly in his wolfish form, he wins over the self-centered popular girl, and he completely alienates his true friends. Eventually, Scott realizes that being a superhuman werewolf isn't all it's cracked up to be and the film concludes with the human Scott playing ball with his team instead of hogging the spotlight to win the big game. Despite playing a high schooler at age twenty-four, there's nothing to dislike about Michael J. Fox. What does set his performance apart from the rest of the lycan hordes is his obvious charm, his fast-changing transformations, and the fact that he's the only film werewolf to date who does an incredible job surfing atop a van!

Jack Nicholson

As mentioned in Chapter 9, there seems to be very little gray area when it comes to Jack Nicholson's performance in the 1994 blockbuster *Wolf.* Some critics opine that Nicholson was simply playing "Nicholson," meaning that his performance was par for the course, while others relent that Nicholson's foray into the movie monster realm is worthy of note. The bottom line is that Nicholson's portrayal of Will Randall, senior editor of a publishing company, is actually atypical for the Oscar-winning actor. Randall is a nice guy, one who's courteous, moral, soft spoken, and low-key—qualities that aren't typically part of Nicholson's acting repertoire. And for the record, *Wolf* still remains the highest grossing werewolf film to date, which just goes to show that critics don't always hold sway over the masses.

After Randall is bitten, he does go through the intoxicating process that comes with gaining superpowers. And though Randall does attack a few humans, his lycanthropy is more in keeping with the reluctant werewolf—only this time with a tidy twist. Early on, Randall seeks out the advice of a renowned expert and professor, Dr. Vijay Alezais (Om Puri). And it's that very conversation with the terminally ill professor that's at the heart of *Wolf*, as he tells Randall about the rules of the werewolf and that "though he consumes, he gives all but his nature and his heart." The professor asserts, "Not all who are bitten change. There must be something wild within—the analog of the wolf." Randall responds by telling him that among his people, "I'm known as the guy least likely to have an analog of the wolf." To this the professor replies, "Your people are wrong, Mr. Randall. Sometimes one doesn't even need to be bitten. Only the passion of the wolf is enough."

The passion of the wolf, in this case, plays out on myriad levels and leaves viewers with the notion that as a werewolf, there are a lot of places you can run but not many in which you can hide from your true self. In many respects, this is Nicholson in one of his better roles, given that sympathetic and successful monsters take a lot of restraint and enormous talent to play convincingly.

Hugh Jackman and Will Kemp

Though director Stephen Sommers's 2004 action-packed horrorfest *Van Helsing* sits firmly in second place on the all-time list of top-grossing vampire flicks having earned over $300 million worldwide to date, it should by rights also be classified as a werewolf film. This fast and furious monster party—which features not only rocking werewolves, but Dracula, Dr. Jekyll, Frankenstein, and Igor—shows Gabriel Van Helsing (played by Australian actor Hugh Jackman) in the secret employ of the Vatican during the late 1800s, as a somewhat conflicted troubadour of the underworld.

As a hired gun, Van Helsing has the unenviable job of hunting Count Dracula (Richard Roxburgh) with the help of gypsy princess Anna Valerious (Kate Beckinsale), while at the same time trying to save her brother Velkan (Will Kemp) from his lycanthropic curse. In what proves to be an epic battle of werewolf versus vampire, Van Helsing embraces his recently acquired lycanthropy—the result of being bitten by Velkan—for the sole purpose of killing Dracula. And he does so in stunning fashion in one of the most memorable werewolf movie scenes of all time (see Chapter 9).

The epitome of a reluctant werewolf, Velkan undergoes an extremely traumatic process of transformation that is equally mesmerizing to watch, but his morphing is riddled with absolute frenzy and panic. A classically trained ballet dancer, British actor Will Kemp shows incredible flexibility and movement, which only makes him that much more believable when we see him tear the clothes and skin from his body in a symbolic measure of unleashing his inner beast.

In both Jackman and Kemp, we see and feel the complexity of the voluntary and reluctant lycanthrope, and above all, the aspect that the good in a man's heart can overpower the evil of his dreaded curse. Though he staunchly fights off his emerging werewolf characteristics, Van Helsing must ultimately embrace the curse, and *that* is what makes him a voluntary werewolf (see Chapter 4). Velkan is the polar opposite. He's spent his entire life fighting Dracula and his lycan minions and, as a result of that battle, becomes the consummate reluctant werewolf. After seeing that Dracula turned his now-deceased father into a werewolf, Velkan's horror and his apprehension become downright explosive.

More so than most horror flicks, *Van Helsing* benefits from an atypical abundance of classic movie monster subtext, including social ostracism, isolation, mortality versus immortality, regeneration and heritage, heaven and hell, psychological torment, and good versus evil. It's impossible *not* to focus on those aspects considering the lineup of monsters who are featured—especially the werewolves. In regard to Van Helsing and Velkan, there is no doubt that the film follows certain aspects of werewolf mythology, especially the skin-dissolving transformations from man to werewolf. Another highly unique aspect of both Van Helsing and Velkan's transformations is when lycans, they both suddenly revert back to their human form if the full moon is hidden behind cloud cover. Once the clouds pass, they immediately resume their lycan form. Amid the chaos of battle throughout the film, that issue is an exceptionally cool twist to the werewolf legend.

What is also unusual is that, unlike most cinematic werewolves, Van Helsing is actually cured of his lycanthropy. As it turns out, a rumor suggesting that Dracula possesses a cure for werewolfism is not only true—it's his big "secret" that he keeps locked up. Why, you ask? Because despite the fact that the Count has been using werewolves to do his bidding for years, a werewolf who has the strength and will to turn on the father of all bloodsuckers can actually kill him. Should Dracula sense that he's in danger, he'd need a serum to change the rebellious werewolf back into a human. In this case, Van Helsing benefits from Dracula's obsessive precaution in the film's climax.

Without question, Hugh Jackman and Will Kemp play their respective werewolf personas paws and claws above the majority of silver screen lupines. Their transformations are fast, furious, and mind-blowing, and are easily some of the best we've ever had the privilege of witnessing. There should be no doubt that both have earned their spots in the werewolf Hall of Fame.

Paul Naschy

True fans of the horror genre will no doubt be familiar with Paul Naschy, whose real name is Jacinto Molina. If you're not, you may be surprised to learn that Naschy has played a werewolf in film more than any other actor. It's true. The Spanish actor and his legendary werewolf alter ego Count Waldemar Daninsky are the Jason Vorhees of the werewolf genre. Naschy has reprised his role of the count twelve times from 1968 to 2003, with the Spanish horror master showing no signs of letting up at the age of seventy-five! Naschy, who is a mainstay in the horror genre, has close to 100 film and television credits to his name and has over the years played a host of famed horror monsters, including Count Dracula, The Mummy, Igor,

Fu Manchú, Satan, medieval warlock Alaric de Marnac, and the Barón Gilles de Lancré, a character based on the infamous thirteenth-century French nobleman, vampire, and convicted serial killer, Gilles de Rais.

What makes Naschy one of the lycan Hall of Famers, aside from his sheer endurance in the genre, is the fact that he doesn't play Daninsky exactly the same way in any film. In fact, the dozen Daninsky films—a number of which Naschy himself penned—called the *Hombre Lobo* series are unique in the history of werewolf cinema. Each outing is seemingly unrelated to its previous storyline. Beginning in 1968, the Daninsky *Hombre Lobo* series of films include (in their English translation):

- *The Mark of the Wolfman* (1968)
- *Nights of the Werewolf* (1968)
- *The Monsters of Terror* (1970)
- *Shadow of the Werewolf* (1971)
- *The Fury of the Wolfman* (1972)
- *Dr. Jekyll and the Wolfman* (1972)
- *Return of the Werewolf* (1973)
- *Night of the Howling Beast* (1975)
- *Return of the Wolfman* (1981)
- *The Werewolf and the Magic Sword* (1983)
- *The Moonlight Murders* (1996)
- *Tomb of the Werewolf* (2004)

Naschy also played a werewolf in the 1982 film *Goodnight, Mr. Monster*, and the 1987 film *Howl of the Devil*, which he not only wrote and directed, but played eight different roles, including Frankenstein, Mr. Hyde, the Phantom of the Opera, Quasimodo, the devil, *and* Count Daninsky! In total, Naschy has played a werewolf fourteen times over the course of thirty-six years. Is he the ultimate howling bad boy werewolf, or what?

Female Fido Hall of Fame

Unlike the vampire realm, there are very few women who suffer the cinematic curse of the werewolf. Why is that, you ask?

Could it be that no one wants to see an excessively hairy gal who has massive amounts of drool dripping down her fangs sprouting a tail? That's one plausible explanation. Is another distinct possibility the fact that female wolves are actually quite loving and maternal? Most definitely! Or is it that the "beast within" just doesn't apply to the "fairer sex"? Let's hope not! That said, there are three werewolf films that benefit from their she-beasts, each one portraying the female werewolf in very different and creative ways.

Full Moon Madness

Do you think I *like* being part of this family? Do you think I chose to run with the pack? No! I chose you. But now you're out of luck and I'm out of time. And all we can do is let nature take its course. They were always here. I just unlocked the door . . . it's *that* time of the month.

—Emma Cleasby as Megan, just prior to transforming into a werewolf in *Dog Soldiers* (2002)

Emma Cleasby

The third lycan Hall of Famer from *Dog Soldiers* is Emma Cleasby, who portrays Megan, the mysterious young zoologist who rescues the hapless soldiers from the remote woods of the Scottish Highlands during a werewolf attack and offers them shelter in a farmhouse belonging to a local family. Though we never actually see Megan transform, she's in many ways the most lethal of the cinematic female lupines. Surrounded by frenzied military hotshots and all the testosterone one expects from highly trained soldiers, she plays her part as the soldier's rescuer and fulfills her role as a dutiful wolf pack member with haunting and devious restraint. Her goal, as we come to find out, is simple: Bring food to her family. It's a goal that she admirably achieves by the film's end by letting her fully transformed werewolf family into the house. She literally lets the devil in the door.

Though Megan is shot in the head just as she begins her transformation, her glowing eyes are enough to make the hair on the back of your neck stand up. The same goes for the hair of the remaining soldiers, who must horrifyingly come to grips with the fact that their perceived savior has, all along, been their greatest enemy. It's a brilliant plot twist, and Cleasby plays her part with such ease that her insipid betrayal elicits both sympathy and a hearty chuckle when she admits that she *had* to let her werewolf family into the house because it's "that time of the month."

Emily Perkins and Katharine Isabelle

If there's one lycan concept that oddly sanctifies the true meaning of supernatural sisterhood it is, without a doubt, the *Ginger Snaps* trilogy. Sisters Brigitte and Ginger Fitzgerald, played by Emily Perkins and Katharine Isabelle, are nothing less than perfect in the Canadian indie trilogy, which is deserving of the cult classic status and awards it has achieved. The utterly morose sisters are alternately dead serious or seriously deadpan in their dark humor, which gives the first offering, *Ginger Snaps*, a brilliant realism despite its highly unrealistic scenario. Both Brigitte and Ginger are heroines, but ultimately it's younger sister Brigitte who shines in all three films as her lycanthropy comes to prominence. In *Ginger Snaps*, Brigitte, realizing that Ginger has indeed begun to "snap," goes into a mode that appears to blend Florence Nightingale and Miss Marple. She tracks Ginger's recently begun menstrual cycle against the lunar cycle, and she enlists the help of a local greenhouse hunk in an effort to concoct a cure from Mom's dried monkshood flowers before her dear sis turns into the same type of snarling mutated mauler who attacked and infected her (see Chapter 4).

Aside from the subtext of social ostracism, defiance, puberty, and teen angst, the power of the human family as well as wolf pack dynamics also come into play. In the first and third film, Brigitte intentionally infects herself with Ginger's blood to prove her devotion to her werewolf sister and their own private wolf pack. Never once does Brigitte doubt or defy her love for Ginger or their motto: "Out by sixteen or dead in the scene. Together forever."

What's even more unique about the trilogy is that each installment approaches the werewolf legend from a different angle. *Ginger Snaps* sets the base for the sisters' relationship by establishing their issues and love despite Ginger's death at the hands of Brigitte. *Ginger Snaps: Unleashed* focuses on Brigitte's fight to stave off her lycanthropic condition with the help of a ghostly Ginger and injections of liquid monkshood (see Chapter 5). *Ginger Snaps Back: The Beginning* takes a surprising turn as the film is set in 1815 at a remote trading fortress in Canada, which is under siege by werewolves called wendigos. As if coming full circle despite the time warp, Brigitte again infects herself with Ginger's blood, which goes to prove that when family is concerned, blood *is* thicker than water. Winner of several awards, the *Ginger Snaps* trilogy is well worth a look as it drives home the brilliance of a wretched animalistic curse, the plight of coming of age, the duty of family, and ultimately, the dark humor of a situation that a pair of wannabe goth sisters *never* saw coming.

Agnes Bruckner

As far as female howlers go, there's one more gal worthy of the lycan Hall of Fame: Agnes Bruckner, who plays teen werewolf Vivian in director Katja von Garnier's 2007 film *Blood and Chocolate*. At first thought, a writer or filmmaker would likely never concoct a werewolf tale with a strong *Romeo and Juliet* subtext. While it's true that *Blood and Chocolate* didn't rise to the same critical acclaim as other werewolf films, it does have a lead female lycan who dares to break from the pack in grand, if not warlike, fashion—and that sets Bruckner apart from the majority of cinematic she-beasts.

As mentioned in Chapter 1, wolves are much like humans in regard to family dynamics. The difference with Vivian is that she's special. She comes from a long line of Romanian loup-garou leaders, and she is part of a prophecy that promises that, as a chosen one, she's also to become the leader of the pack. Given the seriousness and hierarchy of the pack and its current leader, she's got big paws to fill. As fate would have it, falling in love with a human isn't part of the plan. But as rebellious young girls are prone to do, Vivian does what she believes is right. After all, pack leader Gabriel tells her that she has no family (her lycan parents and siblings were slain), only a 5,000-year heritage of loup-garou generations who've managed to co-habitate among humans. But what if one refuses to accept that heritage?

In a werewolf version of *Romeo and Juliet*, Aidan and Vivian must overcome several major hurdles, one being the fact that during a human "hunt," Aidan mistakenly slashes Vivian's paw with a silver dinner knife. With the silver poisoning her blood, he takes the opportunity to test her resolve: He cuts his arm and asks how she feels when smelling his blood. When she admits that she feels fear, he asks if it's the fear of what she'll do to him. Her response? "Fear of what you'll *think* of me." In a film with a few plot holes, that scene stands at the precipice of their tragic love story. Will they or won't they overcome the odds? In this case, after getting Vivian a serum to reverse the effects of the silver, Aidan takes on Gabriel and his pack and in true underdog fashion manages to slay the demon *and* get the girl.

New Fangs on the Block

The fact that cinematic werewolves are on the rise is evidenced in two major movie releases planned for the fall of 2009. The first is what's said to be a remake of Lon Chaney Jr.'s 1941 portrayal of Lawrence Talbot in *The Wolf Man*. Taking on the daunting lycanthropic task of portraying Larry Talbot, and donning what's sure to be top-notch makeup permeated by special effects, is Oscar-winning actor Benicio Del Toro. Rumor has it that several of *The Wolf Man's* original characters will be returning, such as Larry's father, Sir John Talbot (Anthony Hopkins); Gwen Conliffe (Emily Blunt), and gypsy woman Maleva (Geraldine Chaplin). How the updated storyline plays out has yet to be seen, but the mere fact that the penultimate werewolf film is being revisited tells you that as a genre, loony lupines aren't disappearing into the forest anytime soon.

Also coming to the silver screen is the second installment of Stephenie Meyer's *Twilight* series. Unlike the 2008 film *Twilight*, which focuses primarily on the relationship between human teen Bella Swan (Kristen Stewart) and vampire Edward Cullen (Robert Pattinson), *The Twilight Saga: New Moon* will highlight Native American werewolf Jacob Black, played in both films by Taylor Lautner. Given that *Twilight* has become the highest grossing vampire film to date, bringing in close to $380 million thus far according to Box Office Mojo, no doubt its sequel will bode well for the werewolf genre. What will also help bring fans to the theater is the recent casting of Dakota Fanning as a Volturi vampire and Michael Sheen as the all-powerful Volturi leader, Aro.

Silver Screen Skinwalkers

Are you feeling happy after learning about all the best cinematic werewolves? Well, we're just getting started! Though it's admittedly quite difficult to pick your favorite silver screen bad boy, you've now got a better way to find all the werewolf flicks you could ever hope to indulge in from the first silent adaptations to the classics to the cheesy and comedic to the downright spectacular. In Chapters 11 and 12 you'll find a two-part filmography that will, without a doubt, entice your love for all things furry, fanged, and ferociously romantic.

Chapter 11

Reel-Time:
The Silent Era Through
the Big Bad Seventies

For more than eighty years, the mov-
ie-making industry has produced all
measure of films in the horror genre, and a large
and historically significant part of that body
of work involves films focused on werewolves.
From the Silent Era to the present day, we've
been treated to a variety of lupines, from the
dramatic to the spooky to the downright comedic. No matter the decade, each of the following
films has made a contribution to wolf-men and
she-beasts, paying homage to some measure of
myth, legend, and literature. But these films primarily showcase the creative minds of writers,
filmmakers, makeup artists, and special effects
technicians who've conjured up some of the hip-
pest, horrifying, and engaging werewolves the
world has ever seen.

Beastly Cinema

In perusing this two-part werewolf filmography, you may be surprised by the wide range of storylines they follow, from those building off the 1941 film *The Wolf Man* to artistic spin-offs, action-adventure extravaganzas, foreign interpretations, and even a handful of films built off lycan mythology and literature. It must be said that for the purposes of this guide, a select group of films is highlighted to give you an inkling of the full range of creative efforts filmmakers have worked hard to present, from short films to formidable full-blown, big-budget epics. In this chapter we focus on films from the Silent Era through the 1970s, while in Chapter 12 you can peruse films from the 1980s through the new millennium.

Silent Screams to Classic Canines: Let the Howling Begin!

As you've already learned in Chapter 8, 1941 marked ground zero for werewolf cinema with the arrival of Universal's *The Wolf Man*, where we first met Lon Chaney Jr.'s now famous reluctant werewolf Lawrence Talbot. Chaney played the role in five films from 1941 to 1948, including *The Wolf Man*, *Frankenstein Meets the Wolf Man*, *House of Frankenstein*, *House of Dracula*, and *Abbott and Costello Meet Frankenstein*. Those efforts earned the Wolf Man a place in the coveted golden horror triad alongside Dracula and Frankenstein.

After *Wolf Man* premiered, a flood of films were produced whose storylines attempted to capture the same depth and ambiance of Chaney Jr.'s werewolf. Some, you would no doubt find amusing today, like the 1942 film *The Mad Monster* with its mad scientist (George Zucco) and hulking, slow-talking handyman (Glenn Strange), who's given injections of wolf blood and then gleefully watched by the mad doctor as he goes prancing about the swampland as a werewolf killing the locals. It's a nice play on the title, as you don't really know *which* mad monster the filmmakers are referring to—the scientist or the unwilling howling handyman! Worthy of note is that Glenn Strange played the Frankenstein Monster in three of Lon Chaney Jr.'s werewolf outings, including *House of Dracula*, *House of Frankenstein*, and *Abbott and Costello Meet Frankenstein*.

Also premiering in the 1940s is *She-Wolf of London*, a turn-of-the-century murder mystery that has Scotland Yard in a tizzy over bizarre murders being committed in the park by an alleged werewolf. June Lockhart plays heiress Phyllis Allenby, whose family lineage is said to be plagued by lycanthropy. Believing herself to be the She-Wolf, she grows increasingly disturbed, provoking her cousin and aunt to become convinced that she's falling victim to the dreaded curse of the Allenbys. As a contributor to the werewolf genre, *She-Wolf* is actually a nice example of someone suffering clinical lycanthropy (see Chapter 5).

The 1950s experienced a lull in lycan cinema, with one small exception that came in the form of the actor who would become legendary for his television roles of Little Joe Cartwright in *Bonanza*, and Pa Ingalls in *Little House on the Prairie*. Believe it or not, Michael Landon transformed himself into teenage lycan Tony Rivers in the 1957 film *I Was a Teenage Werewolf*. Directed by Gene Fowler Jr., the film, which can easily be described as a combination of *The Wolf Man* meets *The Mad Monster* meets *Rebel Without a Cause*, is the first werewolf movie directed at the teen market, a fact most likely attributed to the drive-in movie era that attracted teens by the droves.

On the Prowl

THE RADIANCE WAS that of the full, setting, and blood-red moon, which now shone vividly through that once barely-discernible fissure ... extending from the roof of the building, in a zigzag direction, to the base.

—Edgar Allan Poe, American author

Though clearly a B-movie classic, what makes Landon's role crucial is that the film, for the conservative 1950s, was heavily marketed, which even led the government to investigate given the overwhelming concern that it would cause further rebellion in teens of the era. That move, of course, backfired as youngsters flocked to the drive-in to watch Landon in action. On that account, he didn't disappoint. As a disagreeable teen prone to violence, Tony Rivers is sent to Dr. Alfred Brandon (Whit Bissell), a shrink who, as luck would have it, turns out to be a mad scientist. Through hypnosis and narcotics Brandon taps into Tony's inner beast and brings forth a werewolf. Bad plan. Murders ensue and Tony becomes a wanted werewolf hell-bent on revenge against his dear doctor. With a subtext of puberty, teen angst, and good versus evil, *Teenage Werewolf* helps further the genre in that scores of future lycan films would focus on the very same teenage traumas.

Here now are the beginnings of werewolf cinema from the Silent Era through the fabulous fifties:

- *The Werewolf* (1913) Clarence Burton, Marie Walcamp, Phyllis Gordon
- *The White Wolf* aka *The White Hunter* (1914)
- *Le loup-garou* aka *The Werewolf* (1923, France) Pierre Bressol, Madeleine Guitty, Jeanne Delvair
- *La loba* aka *She Wolf* (1924, Argentina) Félix Blanco, Gloria Ferrandiz, Argentino Gómez
- *Wolf Blood* aka *Wolfblood: A Tale of the Forest* (1925) Marguerite Clayton, George Chesebro, Ray Hanford
- *Gehetzte Menschen* aka *Loup-Garou* aka *Hunted Men* aka *Werewolf* (1932, Germany) Magda Sonja, Vladimir Sokoloff
- *Werewolf of London* aka *Unholy Hour* (1935) Henry Hull, Warner Oland, Valerie Hobson, Lester Matthews, J. M. Kerrigan
- *The Wolf Man* (1941) Lon Chaney Jr., Claude Rains, Bela Lugosi, Ralph Bellamy, Maria Ouspenskaya
- *The Mad Monster* aka *The Mad Monsters* (1942) Johnny Downs, George Zucco, Anne Nagel

- *The Undying Monster* aka *The Hammond Mystery* (1942) Heather Angel, James Ellison, Bramwell Fletcher
- *Frankenstein Meets the Wolf Man* (1943) Lon Chaney Jr., Bela Lugosi, Lionel Atwill, Patric Knowles, Ilona Massey, Maria Ouspenskaya
- *Le loup des Malveneur* aka *The Wolf of the Malveneurs* (1943) Madeleine Sologne, Pierre Renoir, Gabrielle Dorziat
- *The Three Stooges Meet the Wolf Man* aka *Idle Roomers* (1943) Curly Howard, Larry Fine, Moe Howard, Duke York
- *Cry of the Werewolf* (1944) Nina Foch, Stephen Crane, Osa Massen
- *House of Frankenstein* (1944) Boris Karloff, Lon Chaney Jr., John Carradine
- *The Return of the Vampire* (1944) Nina Foch, Frieda Inescort, Bela Lugosi
- *House of Dracula* aka *The Wolf Man's Cure* (1945) Lon Chaney Jr., John Carradine, Martha O'Driscoll
- *She-Wolf of London* aka *The Curse of the Allenbys* (1946) Don Porter, June Lockhart, Sara Haden
- *Abbott and Costello Meet Frankenstein* (1948) Bud Abbott, Lou Costello, Lon Chaney Jr., Lenore Aubert, Bela Lugosi
- *The Werewolf* (1956) Steven Ritch, Don Megowan, Joyce Holden
- *Daughter of Dr. Jekyll* (1957) John Agar, Gloria Talbott, Arthur Shields
- *I Was a Teenage Werewolf* (1957) Michael Landon, Yvonne Fedderson, Whit Bissell
- *El castillo de los monstrous* aka *Castle of the Monsters* (1958, Mexico) Antonio Espino, Evangelina Elizondo, Carlos Orellana
- *How to Make a Monster* (1958) Robert H. Harris, Paul Brinegar, Gary Conway
- *Tales of Frankenstein: The Professor* (1958) Anton Diffring, Helen Westcott, Don Megowan
- *El hombre y el monstruo* aka *The Man and the Monster* (1959, Mexico) Enrique Rambal, Abel Salazar, Martha Roth

The 1960s: Curses, *Luchadores,* and Mad Monster Parties!

It was during the Swinging Sixties that werewolf cinema finally began to take off, with a wide range of lycans scaring
the skivvies off unsuspecting audiences. A literal melting pot
of lycanthropy in all its forms, the decade brought us a con-
tingent of classic films, such as *The Curse of the Werewolf* and
Lon Chaney Jr.'s *Face of the Screaming Werewolf,* a pair of *Dr.
Terror's* anthologies, a *Munsters* outing, and even a *Mad Monster
Party* featuring Boris Karloff! It also included a strong showing
of Mexican films featuring legendary *lucha libre* (professional
free-fighting wrestling) heroes Santo and Blue Demon. A bit
campy in their presentation, it's a blast watching the masked
luchadores go snout to snout with the werewolf hordes!

Hammer Films, which utterly dominated the vampire genre
as well as other movie monsters from 1931 until the mid-1970s,
produced their only earnest werewolf flick in 1961. Starring
Oliver Reed, *The Curse of the Werewolf* focuses on Leon Corle-
do (Reed), who's born on the twenty-fifth of December. That
aspect comes from werewolf mythology, in that a child born
on the twenty-fifth of December is automatically cursed (see
Chapter 5). Following Leon's travails from boy to man, the film
chronicles the utter frenzy and true mental and physical impairment of a lifelong werewolf. Even by the film's end, when
being pursued by an entire village, Leon is wise enough to re-
alize that he must be killed either by being burned alive or
shot with silver bullets. What helps *The Curse of the Werewolf*
is its director, Terence Fisher, who was one of Hammer's pre-
mier directors of the era. The film is also loosely based on Guy
Endore's 1933 novel *The Werewolf of Paris* (see Chapter 6).

What must also be noted is that the sixties mark the appearance of werewolf Hall of Famer Paul Naschy and his first
two appearances as Count Waldemar Daninsky in the 1968
films *La marca del Hombre-lobo* (*The Mark of the Wolfman*) and
Las noches del Hombre Lobo (*Nights of the Werewolf,* which is
in dispute regarding its actual release date). No slouch in the
werewolf realm, Naschy has played a lycan more than anyone

in film history, having played Daninsky in a dozen films, and werewolves in two additional movies (see Chapter 10).

That said, here are the films you don't want to miss from the Swinging Sixties:

- *La casa del terror* aka *House of Terror* (1960, Mexico) Germán Valdés, Yolanda Varela, Lon Chaney Jr.
- *The Curse of the Werewolf* aka *The Curse of Siniestro* aka *The Wolfman* (1961, United Kingdom) Clifford Evans, Oliver Reed, Catherine Feller
- *Lycanthropus* aka *Werewolf in a Girl's Dormitory* (1961) Barbara Lass, Carl Schell, Curt Lowens
- *Beauty and the Beast* (1962) Joyce Taylor, Mark Damon, Eduard Franz
- *Frankenstein: El vampiro y compania* aka *Frankenstein: The Vampire and Co.* (1962, Mexico) Manuel "Loco" Valdés, Martha Elena Cervántes
- *Santo vs. las mujeres vampiro* aka *Samson vs. the Vampire Women* (1962, Mexico) Santo, Lorena Velázquez, María Duval
- *Santo en el museo de cera* aka *Samson in the Wax Museum* aka *Santo in the Wax Museum* (1963, Mexico) Santo, Claudio Brook, Norma Mora
- *Ye ban ren lang* aka *Midnight Werewolf* (1963, Hong Kong) Yin Choi Cheung, Tat-wah Cho, Ping Ha
- *The Devil Wolf of Shadow Mountain* (1964) Johnny "Bud" Cardos, Gene Pollock
- *El Castillo de los monstrous* aka *Castle of the Monsters* (1964, Mexico) Diego Barquinero, Pablo Blanco, John Gilmore
- *Face of the Screaming Werewolf* (1964) Lon Chaney Jr., Yerye Beirute, George Mitchell
- *Ursus, il terrore dei kirghisi* aka *Hercules, Prisoner of Evil* aka *Terror of the Kirghiz* (1964, Italy) Reg Park, Mireille Granelli, Ettore Manni
- *Demonio azul* aka *The Blue Demon* (1965, Mexico) Blue Demon, Jaime Fernández, Cesar Gay
- *Dr. Terror's House of Horrors* aka *The Blood Suckers* (1965) Christopher Lee, Peter Cushing, Donald Sutherland

- *El charro de las Calaveras* aka The Cowboy of Calaveras (1965, Mexico) Dagoberto Rodríguez, David Silva, Alicia Caro
- *La loba* aka *The She-Wolf* aka *Los Horrores del bosque negro* (1965, Mexico) Kitty de Hoyos, Joaquín Cordero, Columba Domínguez
- *Munster, Go Home!* (1966) Fred Gwynne, Yvonne De Carlo, Al Lewis, Butch Patrick
- *Dr. Terror's Gallery of Horrors* (1967) Lon Chaney Jr., John Carradine, Rochelle Hudson
- *La marca del Hombre-lobo* aka *The Mark of the Wolfman* (1968, Spain) Paul Naschy, Dianik Zurakowska, Manuel Manzaneque
- *Las noches del Hombre Lobo* aka *Nights of the Werewolf* (1968, Spain) Paul Naschy, Peter Beaumont, Monique Brainville
- *Blood of Dracula's Castle* aka *Dracula's Castle* (1969) Alexander D'Arcy, John Carradine, Paula Raymond
- *Mad Monster Party?* (1969, animated) Boris Karloff, Allen Swift, Phyllis Diller
- *The Maltese Bippy* aka *The Incredible Werewolf Murders* (1969) Dan Rowan, Dick Martin, Carol Lynley, Julie Newmar

The 1970s: Los Lobos on the Loose!

The 1970s provides a wonderful mix of eccentric lycans, including six more Paul Naschy films featuring his fur-fiend Count Waldemar Daninsky, a fun handful of Santo and Blue Demon Mexican werewolf romps, a wide range of foreign films, and a doghouse full of quintessential seventies flicks, including *Cry of the Banshee, Moon of the Wolf, The Boy Who Cried Werewolf, The Werewolf of Washington, The Werewolf of Woodstock, Scream of the Wolf, Death Moon,* and *The Beast Must Die.* As any true horror lover can attest, films of the seventies are nothing if not incredibly distinctive.

What likely plays into the way werewolf cinema is presented, as well as all other genres, is the *Hays Code,* also known as the *Production Code*, which was responsible for film censorship from 1930 to 1968, with the majority of its censoring taking place from the forties through the sixties. In 1968, that code was disbanded in favor of the Motion Picture Association of America (MPAA) rating system we know today. With censorship lifted, films of the seventies and the eighties were allowed to include more violence.

Full Moon Madness

Dr. Vijay Alezais (played by Om Puri): There must be something wild within, an analog of the wolf.

Will Randall (played by Jack Nicholson): Well that lets me out. Among my people I'm know as the guy least likely to have an analog of the wolf.

—From *Wolf* (1994)

One of the more interesting werewolf romps of the decade is the 1975 offering *Legend of the Werewolf*, a film clearly influenced by the classic Hammer Films. Its star, in fact, is one of Hammer's most legendary horror actors, Peter Cushing, who as a rather diligent and cheery police surgeon is compelled to get to the bottom of a series of Parisian murders. One curious link is that the film's writer, Anthony Hinds, also wrote director Terence Fisher's 1961 Hammer film *The Curse of the Werewolf*. Despite official citation, *Legend of the Werewolf* also appears to be loosely based on Guy Endore's novel *The Werewolf of Paris*, which is why there are similar references to myth, legend, and literature.

Legend of the Werewolf—perhaps more so than other werewolf films—channels the stories of Romulus and Remus (see Chapter 1) and Robert Florey's original 1931 treatment for *The Wolf Man* (see Chapter 8) in that *Legend's* protagonist, Etoile (David Rintoul), is an infant taken and raised by the wolves who have slain his parents, and thus becomes a feral wolf boy. As a youngster, he's found by a bizarre traveling circus that capitalizes on his feral nature and makes him an attraction until he's old enough to go out on his own. Ending up in Paris working for a small zoo, Etoile falls in love with a prostitute and, as one might predict, her customers start getting murdered by a mysterious animal. *Legend's* subtext obviously maintains additional themes. In particular, Etoile changes into a werewolf only after surviving puberty, he becomes a werewolf during the nights of the full moon, and his urge to kill is brought on by sexual frustration. For what many consider a B-movie, *Legend* has more lycanthropic depth than the average canine fare.

With that in mind, here now are the werewolf flicks from the Brady Bunch decade:

- *Cry of the Banshee* (1970) Vincent Price, Hilary Dwyer, Carl Rigg
- *Los Monstruos del terror* aka *The Monsters of Terror* aka *Assignment Terror* (1970, Mexico) Michael Rennie, Karin Dor, Paul Naschy
- *Santo and Blue Demon Against the Monsters* aka *Santo el enmascarado de plata y Blue Demon contra los monstrous* (1970, Mexico) Santo, Blue Demon, Jorge Rado
- *The Beast of the Yellow Night* (1971) John Ashley, Mary Wilcox, Leopoldo Salcedo
- *O Homem Lobo* aka *The Werewolf* (1971, Brazil) Lino Braga, Tony Cardi, Osmano Cardoso
- *Shadow of the Werewolf* aka *The Werewolf Versus Vampire Women* aka *La noche de Walpurgis* (1971, Spain) Paul Naschy, Gaby Fuchs, Bárbara Capell
- *Drácula contra Frankenstein* aka *Dracula Against Frankenstein* (1972, Spain) Dennis Price, Howard Vernon, Mary Francis
- *Dr. Jekyll y el Hombre Lobo* aka *Dr. Jekyll and the Wolfman* (1972, Spain) Paul Naschy, Shirley Corrigan, Jack Taylor
- *La Furia del Hombre Lobo* aka *The Fury of the Wolfman* aka *The Wolfman Never Sleeps* (1972, Spain) Paul Naschy, Javier Rivera, Michael Rivers

- *Moon of the Wolf* (1972) David Janssen, Barbara Rush, Bradford Dillman
- *The Rats Are Coming! The Werewolves Are Here!* (1972) Hope Stansbury, Jackie Skarvellis, Noel Collins
- *The Boy Who Cried Werewolf* (1973) Kerwin Mathews, Elaine Devry, Scott Sealey
- *Chabelo y Pepito contra los monstrous* aka *Chabelo and Pepito Against the Monsters* (1973, Mexico) Javier López "Chabelo," Martin Ramos Arévalo, Silvia Pasquel
- *El retorno de Walpurgis* aka *Return of the Werewolf* (1973, Spain) Paul Naschy, Fabiola Falcón, Maritza Olivares
- *The Mini-Munsters* (1973, animated short) Richard Long, Cynthia Adler, Al Lewis
- *Ôkami no monshô* aka *Crest of the Wolf* (1973, Japan) Taro Shigaki, Makoto Fujita, Michiko Honda
- *Santo y Blue Demon contra Drácula y el Hombre Lobo* aka *Santo and Blue Demon vs. Dracula and the Wolfman* (1973, Mexico) Santo, Aldo Monti, Blue Demon
- *The Werewolf of Washington* (1973) Dean Stockwell, Katalin Kallay, Henry Ferrentino
- *The Beast Must Die* aka *Black Werewolf* (1974) Calvin Lockhart, Peter Cushing, Marlene Clark
- *Blood* (1974) Allan Berendt, Hope Stansbury, Patricia Gaul
- *The Deathhead Virgin* (1974) Jock Gaynor, Larry Ward, Diane McBain
- *Scream of the Wolf* (1974) Peter Graves, Clint Walker, Jo Ann Pflug
- *La Maldición de la bestia* aka *Night of the Howling Beast* aka *Horror of the Werewolf* (1975, Spain) Paul Naschy, Grace Mills, Silvia Solar
- *Las alegres vampiras de Vögel* aka *Vampires of Vogel* (1975, Spain) J. Alonso Vaz, María José Cantudo, Germán Cobos
- *Legend of the Werewolf* aka *Plague of the Werewolves* (1975) Peter Cushing, Ron Moody, Hugh Griffith
- *Nazareno Cruz y el lobo* aka *The Nazarene Cross and the Wolf* (1975, Argentina) Juan José Camero, Marina Magali, Alfredo Alcón

- *Quem Tem Medo de Lobisomem?* aka *Who's Afraid of the Werewolf?* (1975, Brazil) Reginaldo Faria, Stepan Nercessian
- *The Werewolf of Woodstock* (1975) Tige Andrews, Belinda Balaski, Meredith McRae
- *Santo contra las lobas* aka *Santo vs. the She-Wolves* (1976, Mexico) Santo, Rodolfo de Anda, Gloria Mayo
- *Halloween with the New Addams Family* (1977) John Astin, Alice Fries, Carolyn Jones, Jackie Coogan
- *Darwaza* aka *The Door India* (1978, India) Anil Dhawan, Shyamalee, Imtiaz Khan, Anju Mahendru
- *Death Moon* (1978) Robert Foxworth, Joe Penny, Barbara Trentham
- *O Coronel e o Lobisomem* aka *The Colonel and the Werewolf* (1979, Brazil) Maurício do Valle, Maria Cláudia, Cléa Simões
- *Wolfman* (1979) Earl Owensby, Kristina Reynolds, Julian Morton

Cry Wolf

The first six decades of werewolf cinema gave filmmakers a strong base from which to work their lycanthropic magic. Where that really pays off is in modern-day films, when ever-improving special effects and higher production budgets have progressively accelerated werewolves to spectacular creatures who, even on their bad hair days, surpass the majority of classic movie monster transformations. With that in mind, let's look through the pages of new-age werewolf films and all the fun, fangs, fur, and fantasy they provide.

Chapter 12

Reel-Time :
The Eighties Through
the New Millennium

Since the Silent Era, as highlighted in Chapter 11, the cinematic lycan has experienced a wild and varied evolution that picked up steam as we entered into the sixties and seventies. Now we're moving on to modern-day werewolves, when the untamed bad boys and she-beasts began to truly bust out of their skin with fantastic performances, more elaborate plotlines, and more impressive special effects! If the films of the eighties, nineties, and the new millennium prove anything, it's that once you let the werewolves out—there's no getting them back in the cage!

Modern-Day Werewolves

While many legendary movie monsters have continued a steady pace in the horror genre, werewolves have had a slow buildup that only in the past thirty years has begun to show signs of true horror immortality. In the eighties and nineties the number of werewolf flicks doubled from that of the sixties, and it has doubled again since the year 2000. That increase could be due to several factors, including the invention of the VCR, DVDs, cable and satellite abilities, DVRs, and the chance to watch great flicks over and over. Another probability is the gamble filmmakers and their financial backers are willing to take on potential big-budget blockbusters like *Van Helsing* and *Underworld: Evolution*, which have worldwide grosses of more than $300 million and $111 million respectively. That said, let's take a gander at the films of the past three decades and issue a collective howl at the moon in tribute to the creative and astonishing werewolves that have captured our collective imagination.

The 1980s: Bad Moons, Campy Canines, and Lunar Lunacy

Coming off a decade of decidedly wacky lycans, the eighties were primed and ready for a resurgence of snarling werewolves the likes of which we'd never before seen. And guess what? That's exactly what we got. In 1981, *Wolfen, The Howling*, and *An American Werewolf in London* literally turned around the entire werewolf genre (see Chapter 9). In the case of the latter two, they set the new standard for lycan transformation with *Howling's* Eddie Quist (Robert Picardo) and *American Werewolf* David Kessler (David Naughton) skyrocketing to the lycan Hall of Fame (see Chapter 10). One of the links between the two films? Legendary makeup and special effects artist Rick Baker, who won an Oscar for *American Werewolf*. In addition, *The Howling* launched what is the most successful and prolific franchise in werewolf history, with six sequels from 1985 to 1995, three of which premiered in the eighties.

In 1984, director Neil Jordan brought to life an amalgam of lycan lore and Freudian coming of age tales in *The Company of Wolves*, the first contemporary offering of *Little Red Riding Hood*, starring Sarah Patterson and Angela Lansbury as the Granny. The following year, in 1985, we were treated to *Stephen King's Silver Bullet*, complete with a demented werewolf preacher; the romantic *Ladyhawke*; and the fifth top-grossing werewolf flick of all time—the eternally comedic *Teen Wolf*.

ℱull Moon Madness

Never stray from the path, never eat a windfall apple, and never trust a man whose eyebrows meet in the middle.

—Angela Lansbury as Granny in *The Company of Wolves* (1994)

From there on out, the eighties brought us three *Howling* sequels, a *Teen Wolf* sequel, a classic *Scooby Doo*, an Isabella Rossellini version of *Red Riding Hood*, and two more Paul Naschy outings, one of which proved astonishing. In the 1987 film *El aullido del diablo*, or *Howl of the Devil*, the ultimate Spanish silver screen werewolf played not one but *eight* different roles, including classic monsters *and* famed Count Waldemar Daninsky. Now how's that for dedication to the genre? (See Chapter 10.)

Here are some of the fabulous films of the eighties:

* *Hammer House of Horror: Children of the Full Moon* (1980, United Kingdom) Christopher Cazenove, Celia Gregory, Diana Dors
* *The Monster Club* (1980) Vincent Price, John Carradine, Anthony Steel, Roger Sloman

- *An American Werewolf in London* (1981) David Naughton, Jenny Agutter, Griffin Dunne
- *El retorno del Hombre-Lobo* aka *Night of the Werewolf* aka *Return of the Wolfman* (1981, Spain) Silvia Aguilar, Pilar Alcón, Luis Barboo
- *Full Moon High* (1981) Adam Arkin, Ed McMahon, Roz Kelly
- *The Howling* (1981) Dee Wallace, Patrick Macnee, Dennis Dugan, John Carradine
- *The Munsters' Revenge* (1981) Fred Gwynne, Al Lewis, Yvonne De Carlo
- *Wolfen* (1981) Albert Finney, Edward James Olmos, Gregory Hines, Diane Venora
- *The Beast Within* (1982) Ronny Cox, Bibi Besch, Paul Clemens
- *Buenas noches, señor monstruo* aka *Goodnight, Mr. Monster* (1982, Spain) Regaliz, Fernando Bilbao, Paul Naschy
- *Coming Soon* (1982, documentary) Narrated by Jamie Lee Curtis, focusing on the fifty greatest horror films by Universal Pictures.
- *Cazador de demonios* aka *Demon Hunter* (1983, Mexico) Rafael Sánchez Navarro, Tito Junco, Roxana Chávez
- *La bestia y la espada mágica* aka *The Werewolf and the Magic Sword* (1983, Spain) Paul Naschy, Julia Saly, Beatriz Escudero
- *Conquest* aka *Mace the Outcast* (1983, Italy) Jorge Rivero, Andrea Occhipinti, Conrado San Martin
- *Thriller* aka *Michael Jackson's Thriller* (1983) Michael Jackson, Ola Ray, Forrest J. Ackerman, Rick Baker
- *The Company of Wolves* (1984) Angela Lansbury, Sarah Patterson, David Warner
- *Kaos* aka *Chaos* (1984, Italy) Claudio Bigagli, Enrica Maria Modugno, Massimo Bonetti
- *Leviatán* aka *Monster Dog* (1984, Spain) Alice Cooper, Victoria Vera, Carlos Santurio
- *Tales of the Third Dimension* (1984) Robert Bloodworth, Kevin Campbell, William T. Hicks
- *The Adventures of a Two-Minute Werewolf* (1985) Knowl Johnson, Julia Reardon, Melba Moore, Lainie Kazan

- *Howling II: Your Sister Is a Werewolf* (1985) Christopher Lee, Annie McEnroe, Reb Brown
- *Ladyhawke* (1985) Rutger Hauer, Michelle Pfeiffer, Matthew Broderick
- *The Midnight Hour* aka *In the Midnight Hour* (1985) Jonelle Allen, Lee Montgomery, Shari Belafonte, LeVar Burton, Peter DeLuise
- *Silver Bullet* aka *Stephen King's Silver Bullet* (1985) Gary Busey, Everett McGill, Corey Haim, Terry O'Quinn
- *Teen Wolf* (1985) Michael J. Fox, James Hampton, Susan Ursitti
- *Transylvania 6-5000* (1985) Jeff Goldblum, Geena Davis, Joseph Bologna, Carol Kane
- *Banpaia hantâ D* aka *Vampire Hunter D* (1985, Japanese anime) Kaneto Shiozawa, Michael McConnohie, Ichirô Nagai
- *Deadtime Stories* (1986) Scott Valentine, Nicole Picard, Matt Mitler
- *Haunted Honeymoon* (1986) Gildra Radner, Gene Wilder, Dom DeLuise, Jonathan Pryce
- *Teen Wolf* aka *The Cartoon Adventures of Teen Wolf* (1986, animated) Townsend Coleman, James Hampton, Don Most
- *El aullido del diablo* aka *Howl of the Devil* (1987, Spain) Paul Naschy, Isabel Prinz, Fernando Hilbeck
- *The Howling III* aka *Howling III: The Marsupials* (1987) Barry Otto, William Yang, Imogen Annesley
- *La croce dalle sette pietre* aka *Cross of the Seven Jewels* (1987, Italy) Marco Antonio Andolfi, Annie Belle, Gordon Mitchell
- *The Monster Squad* (1987) Andre Gower, Robby Kiger, Stephen Macht
- *Teen Wolf Too* (1987) Jason Bateman, Kim Darby, John Astin
- *Werewolf* (1987, television series) John J. York, Lance LeGault, Chuck Connors
- *Fright Night Part 2* (1988) Roddy McDowall, William Ragsdale, Julie Carmen
- *Howling IV: The Original Nightmare* (1988) Romy Windsor, Michael T. Weiss, Antony Hamilton

- *Lone Wolf* (1988) Dyan Brown, Ann Douglas, Kevin Hart
- *The Night of the Living Duck* (1988, animated) Mel Blanc, Mel Tormé
- *Scooby-Doo and the Reluctant Werewolf* (1988, animated) Don Messick, Casey Kasem, Rob Paulsen
- *Howling V: The Rebirth* (1989) Philip Davis, Victoria Catlin, Elizabeth Shé
- *My Mom's a Werewolf* (1989) Susan Blakely, John Saxon, Tina Caspary, John Schuck, Ruth Buzzi, Marcia Wallace
- *Night Shadow* (1989) Tom Boylan, Laura Graham, Kato Kaelin
- *Red Riding Hood* (1989) Amelia Shankley, Isabella Rossellini, Craig T. Nelson

Full Moon Madness

Larry Talbot (played by Lon Chaney Jr.): You don't understand. Every night when the moon is full I turn into a wolf!

Wilbur Grey (played by Lou Costello): You and 20 million other guys.

—From *Abbott and Costello Meet Frankenstein* (1948)

The 1990s: Moonrakers and Hair-Raising Howlers!

Of all the decades of lycan cinema, the nineties is arguably one of the most varied in that it highlights a handful of sequels, several notable foreign productions, a host of children's stories, and a number of offbeat films based on the werewolf mystique, including director Tim Burton's *The Nightmare Before Christ-*

mas, Mario Van Peebles in *Full Eclipse*, Mariel Hemingway in *Bad Moon, Halloweentown*, two more *Howling* sequels, and a pair of *Munsters* comedies. What also emerged from the nineties is the number one highest grossing werewolf flick of all time: director Mike Nichols's 1994 film *Wolf*, starring Jack Nicholson, Michelle Pfeiffer, and James Spader, which to date has pulled in close to $132 million worldwide (see Chapters 9 and 10).

One underrated werewolf film is the 1992 Mary Stuart Masterson and Hart Bochner flick *Mad at the Moon*, one of the few western werewolf movies that's worth a look. Beautifully filmed with an exquisite musical score, the storyline focuses on Jenny Hill (Masterson), who forgoes marrying her true love, outlaw James Miller (Stephen Blake). Instead, she's pressured by her family to marry Miller's reserved half-brother, Miller Brown (Bochner), who's also in love with her. Isolated in a remote cabin, the real fun starts when the already wary Jenny realizes that Miller isn't just her new hubby—he's a werewolf with a penchant for getting awfully noisy by the light of the moon!

Full Moon Madness

I *love* Americans. You all have a good taste.

—Pierro Cosso as Claude in *An American Werewolf in Paris* (1997)

Another gem is the 1999 dark comedy *The Curse*, starring Amy Laughlin and written and directed by Jacqueline Garry. Clearly a low-budget romp, what's amusing about *The Curse* is that, despite being bitten by a rabid werewolf, Laughlin's character, Frida, is convinced that the ill effects she's suffering are the result of severe PMS! Of course, once she starts transforming during the full moon and the men she dates are found mauled to death, the true extent of her affliction kicks in.

On that note, let's take a look at the best films the nineties has to offer:

- *Meridian* aka *Meridian: Kiss of the Beast* (1990) Sherilyn Fenn, Malcolm Jamieson, Charlie Spradling
- *The Runestone* (1990) Peter Riegert, Joan Severance, William Hickey, Alexander Godunov
- *She-Wolf of London* (1990, series) Kate Hodge, Neil Dickson, Dan Gilvezan
- *The Curse of Claudia* (1991) Nathan Schiff, Beverly Colton, Joseph Marzano
- *Howling VI: The Freaks* (1991) Brendan Hughes, Michele Matheson, Sean Gregory Sullivan
- *Mom* (1991) Stella Stevens, Jeanne Bates, Brion James
- *Wolfman Chronicles* aka *Wolfman: A Cinematic Scrapbook* (1991, documentary) Wolfman Jack
- *Mad at the Moon* (1992) Mary Stuart Masterson, Hart Bochner, Stephen Blake, Fionnula Flanagan
- *Monster in My Pocket: The Big Scream* (1992, animated) Marvin Kaplan, Mitzi McCall, Robert Paulsen, Frank Welker
- *Donor Party* (1993, animated short)
- *Full Eclipse* (1993) Mario Van Peebles, Patsy Kensit, Bruce Payne
- *The Nightmare Before Christmas* (1993) Danny Elfman, Chris Sarandon, Catherine O'Hara
- *Conrad Brooks vs. the Werewolf* (1994) Henry Bederski, Conrad Brooks, Ted Brooks, Rocky Nelson
- *Twisted Tales* (1994, anthology) Theresa Oliva, Lawrence McCleery, Joe Mauceri
- *Wolf* (1994) Jack Nicholson, Michelle Pfeiffer, James Spader, Kate Nelligan
- *Here Come the Munsters* (1995) Edward Herrmann, Veronica Hamel, Robert Morse, Christine Taylor, Mathew Botuchis
- *Howling: New Moon Rising* aka *Howling VII: Mystery Woman* (1995) John Ramsden, Ernest Kester, Clive Turner
- *Monster Mash: The Movie* (1995) Ian Bohen, Candace Cameron Bure, John Kassir, Adam Shankman

- *Project: Metalbeast* (1995) Barry Bostwick, Kim Delaney, Kane Hodder, Musetta Vander
- *Shriek of the Lycanthrope* (1995) Anthony Ingoglia, Debbie Rochon, Tina Krause
- *Bad Moon* (1996) Mariel Hemingway, Michael Paré, Mason Gamble
- *Frankenstein and Me* (1996) Jamieson Boulanger, Ricky Mabe, Polly Shannon, Louise Fletcher, Burt Reynolds
- *Lycantropus: The Moonlight Murders* aka *Licántropo: El asesino de la luna llena* (1996, Spain) Paul Naschy, Amparo Muñoz, Antonio Pica
- *The Munsters' Scary Little Christmas* (1996) Sam McMurray, Ann Magnuson, Bug Hall
- *Slaves of the Vampire Werewolf* aka *Blood Slaves of the Vampire Werewolf* (1996) Conrad Brooks, James Chean
- *Werewolf* aka *Arizona Werewolf* (1996) George Rivero, Richard Lynch, Federico Cavalli
- *Wilderness* (1996) Johanna Benyon, Molly Bolt, Mark Caven
- *An American Werewolf in Paris* aka *American Werewolf 2* (1997) Tom Everett Scott, Julie Delpy, Vince Vieluf
- *The Creeps* (1997) Rhonda Griffin, Justin Lauer, Bill Moynihan
- *House of Frankenstein* (1997) Adrian Pasdar, Greg Wise, Teri Polo, Jorja Fox
- *Mortal Kombat: Annihilation* aka *Mortal Kombat 2* (1997) Robin Shou, James Remar, Talisa Soto
- *Goosebumps: The Werewolf of Fever Swamp* (1997) Brendan Fletcher, Maria Ricossa, Mairon Bennett. Based on the book by R. L. Stine.
- *Blue Moon* (1998) Brian Garton, Heather Howe, Amanda Wilburn
- *Halloweentown* (1998) Debbie Reynolds, Judith Hoag, Kimberly J. Brown
- *The Wolfman's Cure: La cura del lupo mannaro* (1998, Italian short)
- *Sieben Monde* aka *Night Time* aka *Seven Moons* (1998, Germany) Jan Josef Liefers, Marie Bäumer, Ulrich Mühe

- *The Werewolf Reborn!* (1998) Ashley Cafagna-Tesora, Robin Atkins Downes, Bogdan Cambera
- *The Wolves of Kromer* (1998) Boy George (narrator), James Layton, Lee Williams
- *Cold Hearts* (1999) Marisa Ryan, Robert Floyd, Amy Jo Johnson
- *The Curse* (1999) Amy Laughlin, Mike Dooly, Sara Elena Knight
- *Eyes of the Werewolf* (1999) Mark Sawyer, Stephanie Beaton, Jason Clark
- *Lycanthrope* aka *Bloody Moon* (1999) Robert Carradine, Michael Winslow, Rebecca Holden
- *Monster by Moonlight! The Immortal Saga of The Wolf Man* (1999, documentary) Rick Baker, John Landis, Curt Siodmak
- *Rage of the Werewolf* (1999) Santo Marotta, Joe Zaso, Debbie Rochon
- *The Unexplained: Witches Werewolves and Vampires, Are They Real?* (1999, documentary) Narrated by Peter Graves.
- *The Wolf Man* (1999, United Kingdom, animated short) Waen Shepherd

The New Millennium: Hip, Hunky, and Horrifically Romantic

The astonishing thing about werewolf cinema in the new millennium is that it has absolutely exploded, with well over seventy films to date. Among them are the crème de la crème of the genre, including The *Underworld* trilogy, *Van Helsing*, the *Ginger Snaps* trilogy, *Le Pacte des Loups* (*Brotherhood of the Wolf*), *Blood and Chocolate*, and *Dog Soldiers*, all of which are part of the lycan Hall of Fame and best werewolf cinema discussed in Chapters 9 and 10. But that's just the tip of the iceberg. There are many more films of this decade, and almost all of them are worth watching!

Those films include *Harry Potter and the Prisoner of Azkaban*, which features legendary lycan Professor Remus Lupin;

the campy outing *The Beast of Bray Road*; the *Kibakichi* and *Vampire Hunter D* Japanese anime films; Heath Ledger in *The Brothers Grimm*; and *Skin Walkers* starring Roxana Zal to name a few. Three films that are particularly intriguing are the 2006 werewolf family dispute *Skinwalkers*, the incredibly campy and hysterical 2005 indie flick *Mexican Werewolf in Texas*, and the Wes Craven film *Cursed*.

Skinwalkers

In our discussion of voluntary werewolves in Chapter 4, you learned about the film *Skinwalkers*, which tells of a lycan family split between its entirely "good" faction and a pack led by a rogue evil family member. The film stars Elias Koteas, Jason Behr, and Rhona Mitra, who plays the coveted role of Lucian's vampiric lover Sonja in *Underworld: Rise of the Lycans* (2009). What makes *Skinwalkers* one of the better werewolf films is that a very distinct and sympathetic pack of lycans effectively mimics the family dynamics of both humans and wolves in the wild. As werewolves, they retain much of their human form—but more importantly their human nature in *not* wanting to intentionally harm anyone. The members of the good lycan faction actually chain themselves to walls during the nights of the full moon, which is unusual in the werewolf realm.

Mexican Werewolf in Texas

With a name like *Mexican Werewolf in Texas*, there's no denying that you'd expect an eccentric lycan flick worthy of B-movie status and, on that account, you'd be correct. *Mexican Werewolf* is definitely an indie film, but in the werewolf cinematic realm it defies the norm in that its slobbering, vicious werewolf is a Mexican *Chupacabra*, a legendary creature that primarily subsists on the blood of goats. What's fun about the film is the havoc wreaked on the middle-of-nowhere town of Furlough, Texas, whose 327-member population includes a group of seriously bored teens who decide to take matters into their own hands and slay the evil werewolf by whatever means necessary. Of course, it doesn't help that Furlough is the self-proclaimed "Goat Capital of the World," and that the chupacabra "werewolf" not only wipes out the goat population, but then starts working on anyone who has animal blood on them. As you can imagine, this doesn't bode well for the town butcher or veterinarian! At its finest, *Mexican Werewolf* is campy and admittedly unintentionally funny, especially when the town mortician hops around the desert in a homemade chupacabra outfit sewn of animal pelts. His intention is not to kill the beast—but rather to get rid of his daughter's boyfriend! As far as traditional werewolves go this drooling hellhound is a great example of one that doesn't respond to traditional methods of slaying, falling squarely into the "mutated mauler" type of werewolf that can typically be destroyed by a number of traditional means and not by the use of silver and fire (see Chapter 4). If you're up for a few chuckles, *Mexican Werewolf in Texas* is well worth a bowl of popcorn.

Wes Craven's Cursed

Ranked eighth on Box Office Mojo's all-time top-grossing werewolf list is *Wes Craven's Cursed* starring Christina Ricci as Ellie and Jesse Eisenberg as her wimpy brother, Jimmy. After being attacked by a werewolf during a car accident, the pair begin exhibiting odd signs of wolfish behavior. Ellie is attracted to the smell of a co-worker's bloody nose while at her job as Craig Kilborn's assistant on his talk show. While at school, Jimmy uncharacteristically pounds the daylights out of a bullying rival on the wrestling mat. Although Jimmy is convinced they're both turning into werewolves, Ellie doesn't quite buy the idea until her boyfriend Jake (Joshua Jackson) finally confesses that *he* is a werewolf. After a series of murders, Jake tries to convince Ellie that they can live side-by-side as werewolves for eternity, but he'll have to kill Jimmy first. In the final harrowing battle, Ellie and Jimmy begin transforming into werewolves, but Jake has the upper hand with more experience, strength, and control. At the last moment, Jimmy distracts Jake long enough to allow Ellie to stab Jake with a silver cake knife, which drops him wounded to the ground. She then lops off his head with a shovel after which his body bursts into flames and disappears in a ball of ashes. In a rare turn of events, Ellie and Jimmy happily return to normal after the curse is broken.

Although *Cursed* is one of the most entertaining werewolf films to hit the silver screen, it experienced a number of setbacks during production and editing. Most critics assert that it's a miracle the film was ever completed. It is directed by Wes Craven with a screenplay by Kevin Williamson, who together created the blockbuster horror romp *Scream*, and was originally intended to have the same campy, over-the-top edginess. Miramax studio was unhappy with the results and forced a number of major changes to the plotline, finally toning the gore down to receive a young adult-friendly PG rating. Regardless, it's worth a look given that few werewolves are *ever* killed with a silver cake knife!

Looking Forward

What we really have to look forward to are a few films scheduled to make their premiere in the fall of 2009. *The Wolf Man* is said to be a remake of the Lon Chaney's 1941 lycanthropic romp and, in that regard, director Joe Johnston and Oscar-winning actor Benicio Del Toro as Lawrence Talbot have a huge challenge ahead of them. How close this version is to the original has yet to be seen, but the fact it's being produced reinforces the fact that pop-culture werewolves are again on the rise. The much-anticipated sequel to Stephenie Meyer's novel adaptation of the best selling *Twilight* saga is also scheduled to be released in the fall. In *The Twilight Saga: New Moon*, werewolf Jacob Black becomes a major player, and will likely remain so for future sequels. How his lycanthropy is presented should prove interesting. Even more intriguing is director Chris Weitz and his producer's efforts to boost the film's credibility by casting renowned child actress Dakota Fanning as a Volturi vampire. But it doesn't stop there. What many experts consider to be an even bigger coup is that *Underworld's* Michael Sheen will trade in his lycan fur for a set of legitimate vampire fangs as *New Moon's* Aro, the Volturi leader of all vampires.

With that in mind, check out the terrific selection of werewolf cinema in the millennium and the lycanthropic flicks we have to look forward to in the upcoming year:

- *Alvin and the Chipmunks Meet the Wolfman* (2000, animated) Ross Bagdasarian Jr., Janice Karman, Maurice LaMarche, Frank Welker
- *Ginger Snaps* (2000, Canada) Emily Perkins, Katharine Isabelle, Kris Lemche, Mimi Rogers
- *Monster Mash* (2000, animated) Scott McNeil, Ian James Corlett, Robert O. Smith
- *Vampire Hunter D: Bloodlust* (2000, Japanese anime) Hideyuki Tanaka, Ichirô Nagai, Kôichi Yamadera
- *Blood of the Werewolf* (2001) Tony Luna, Mia Borrelli, Bruce G. Hallenbeck
- *Le Pacte des Loups* aka *Brotherhood of the Wolf* (2001, France) Samuel Le Bihan, Vincent Cassel, Monica Bellucci, Mark Dacascos
- *Wolf Girl* aka *Blood Moon* (2001, Canada) Shelby Fenner, Shawn Ashmore, Tony Denman
- *Bites: The Werewolf Chronicles* (2002) Jacquie Floyd, Mireille Leveque, Anthony Pereira, Michael McCallum
- *Dog Soldiers* (2002, United Kingdom) Sean Pertwee, Kevin McKidd, Emma Cleasby, Liam Cunningham
- *Lyckantropen* (2002, Sweden) Josefin Adner, Julia Brådhe-Dehnisch, Felix Engström
- *Pistolero* (2002, Philippines) Jeric Raval, John Apacible, Jo Ann Miller
- *Wolves of Wall Street* (2002) William Gregory Lee, Louise Lasser, Jeff Branson, Eric Roberts
- *Dark Wolf* (2003) Samaire Armstrong, Ryan Alosio, Andrea Bogart

- *Exhumed* (2003, Canada) Masahiro Oyake, Hiroaki Itaya, Claire Westby
- *The Tenement* (2003) Carol DiMarsico, Joe Lauria, Mike Lane
- *Underworld* (2003) Kate Beckinsale, Scott Speedman, Michael Sheen, Bill Nighy
- *Weird Stories: Werewolves* (2003) Documentary about werewolf myths and legends.
- *Werewolf Tales* (2003) Randal Malone
- *Evil Deeds* (2004) Brian Ramme, Lynda Huyck, Natalie Fortensky
- *Ginger Snaps: Unleashed* aka *Ginger Snaps 2: Unleashed* (2004, Canada) Emily Perkins, Brendan Fletcher, Katharine Isabelle
- *Ginger Snaps Back: The Beginning* aka *Ginger Snaps 3* (2004, Canada) Katharine Isabelle, Emily Perkins, Nathaniel Arcand
- *Halloweentown High* aka *Halloween III* (2004) Kimberly J. Brown, Debbie Reynolds, Judith Hoag
- *Harry Potter and the Prisoner of Azkaban* (2004) Daniel Radcliffe, Richard Griffiths, David Thewlis
- *I tre volti del terrore* aka *The Three Faces of Terror* (2004) John Phillip Law, Riccardo Serventi Longhi
- *Kibakichi: Bakko-yokaiden* aka *Werewolf Warrior* (2004, Japan) Nozomi Andô, Ryuuji Harada, Tatsuo Higashida
- *Kibakichi: Bakko-yokaiden 2* aka *Kibakichi 2* (2004, Japan) Ryuuji Harada, Miki Tanaka, Masakatsu Funaki
- *Lastikman* (2004, Philippines) Mark Bautista, Sarah Geronimo, Cherie Gil
- *The Lunar Pack* (2004) Melissa Morse, Colleen Kavanaugh, Jason L. Liquori
- *Romasanta* aka *The Werewolf Manhunt* aka *Werewolf Hunter: The Legend of Romasanta* (2004, Spain) Julian Sands, Elsa Pataky, John Sharian
- *Skin Walker* (2004) Roxana Zal, Jesse Camp, Ashley Peldon
- *Tomb of the Werewolf* (2004) Paul Naschy, Jay Richardson, Michelle Bauer

- *Van Helsing* (2004) Hugh Jackman, Kate Beckinsale, Richard Roxburgh
- *The Beast of Bray Road* (2005) Jeff Denton, Tom Downey, Sarah Lieving
- *The Brothers Grimm* (2005) Heath Ledger, Petr Ratimec, Barbara Lukesova, Anna Rust
- *Cursed* aka *Wes Craven's Cursed* (2005) Christina Ricci, Joshua Jackson, Portia de Rossi
- *Full Moon Fallen* (2005, Australian short) Nicholas Torres, Adriana Torres, Louis Perri
- *Mexican Werewolf in Texas* (2005) Erika Fay, Gabriel Gutierrez, Michael Carreo
- *Werewolf in Bangkok* (2005, Thailand) Choosak Iamsook, Debbie Bazoo, Natnicha Cherdchubupakari
- *Wild Country* (2005, Scotland) Samantha Shields, Martin Compston, Peter Capaldi
- *Wolfsbayne* (2005) Jim O'Rear, Gunar Hansen, Linnea Quigley
- *Curse of the Wolf* (2006) Lanny Poffo, Darian Caine, Brian Heffron
- *The Feeding* (2006) Kara Maria Amedon, Sam Blankenship, Barry Ellenberger
- *Full Moon Massacre* (2006, United Kingdom) James D. Messer, Toni Bird, Ken Mood
- *In the Red* (2006) Nick Laden, Jeremy Spencer, Al Berrero, Karen Wallace
- *Lycan Colony* (2006) Sean Burgoyne, Gretchen Weisiger, Bill Sykes
- *Lycanthropy* (2006, United Kingdom) George Calil, Alan Convy, Riana Husselmann
- *Skinwalkers* (2006, Canada) Jason Behr, Elias Koteas, Rhona Mitra
- *Underworld: Evolution* (2006) Kate Beckinsale, Scott Speedman, Tony Curran, Michael Sheen
- *Wolfika* (2006) Lucien Eisenach, Donny Versiga, Jaims Weinbrandt
- *Blood and Chocolate* (2007) Agnes Bruckner, Hugh Dancy, Olivier Martinez

- *Cold Blooded* (2007) Jared Eamon, Matt Hagel, Dan Sorensen
- *Hellboy Animated: Blood and Iron* (2007, animated) Ron Perlman, Selma Blair, John Hurt
- *Hybrid* (2007) Cory Monteith, Tinsel Korey, Justine Bateman
- *The Lycanthrope* (2007) Paul Diomede, Damani Rivers, Jenna Finley
- *Nature of the Beast* (2007) Eddie Kaye Thomas, Autumn Reeser, Eric Mabius
- *Werewolf: The Devil's Hound* aka *Lycan* (2007) Michael Dionne, Tamara Malawitz, Phil Gauvin
- *Beware the Moon: Remembering An American Werewolf in London* (2008, documentary) John Landis, David Naughton, Jenny Agutter, Griffin Dunne
- *Never Cry Werewolf* (2008) Nine Dobrev, Kevin Sorbo, Peter Stebbings
- *There's a Werewolf in My Attic!* (2008) Nadine Gross, Joe Noreen, Lacey Prpic-Hedtke
- *Twilight* (2008) Kristen Stewart, Robert Pattinson, Taylor Lautner
- *The Wimp Whose Woman Was a Werewolf* (2008) Marisa Tomasic, Lloyd Kaufman, Larry Longstreth
- *Neowolf* aka *The Band from Hell* (2009) Agim Kaba, Michael Frascino, Heidi Johanningmeier, Veronica Cartwright
- *The Twilight Saga: New Moon* (2009) Robert Pattinson, Kristen Stewart, Taylor Lautner, Michael Sheen
- *Underworld: Rise of the Lycans* (2009) Michael Sheen, Bill Nighy, Rhona Mitra
- *War Wolves* (2009) John Saxon, Tim Thomerson, Adrienne Barbeau
- *Werewolf Trouble* (2009, short) Charlie Anderson, Ryan Conrath, Matt Lawrence
- *The Wolf Man* (2009) Emily Blunt, Benicio Del Toro, Anthony Hopkins, Hugo Weaving
- *Wolvesbayne* (2009) Mark Dacascos, Jeremy London, Yancy Butler

Future Film Bites

With over 300 films credited to the werewolf genre, it's a sure bet that we haven't seen the last of the silver screen werewolf. Every day new innovations in filmmaking, special effects, makeup, cinematography, and CGI, among many other things, are being instituted, so there should be no doubt that cinematic lycans will only get bigger, bolder, and infinitely more realistic. That said, there is a lot to look forward to in the coming years and plenty of historic films that are sure to make *you* howl at the moon!

Afterword

Shoot for the Moon

I'm afraid we've come to the end of our full moon madness. I do hope that amid the falling leaves and misty sun-drenched forests of myth, legend, literature, and cinema, you've learned that the world of werewolves is just as mysterious as the real wolves who lurk amid the shadows. As a researcher and chronicler, I am like many other literary gypsies, who throughout history alternately hunt or are in league with the creatures of the night. That is, of course, in the metaphorical sense. As an appropriate exit into the eternal mist of the werewolf realm, it's apropos that *The Wolf Man's* spiritual and supernatural sage, Maleva the gypsy woman, has the final word. She spoke this immortal verse to her lycan son Bela and Lawrence Talbot after their deaths:

> *The way you walked was thorny*
> *Through no fault of your own*
> *But as the rain enters the soil*
> *The river enters the sea*
> *So tears run to a predestined end.*
> *Your suffering is over*
> *Now you will find peace for eternity.*

No matter your opinion on the ultimate untamed bad boy, there's no doubt that the plight of the werewolf is more often than not a sympathetic one when viewed by the outsider. If werewolves really do exist, then we can only hope that whatever their transformation or their plight, they ultimately find happiness roaming wild and free amid a forest dappled with light and shade that alternately provides us warmth and, occasionally, a sudden chill. No doubt we'll all pay homage to the werewolf the next time we hear a howl and look up to the heavens to see an unbearably bright, shiny full moon.

Index

About the Author

*B*arb Karg is a twenty-seven-year veteran journalist, author, graphic designer, and screenwriter. A seasoned writer, she has authored or coauthored over two dozen books, including *The Girl's Guide to Vampires*; *The Everything® Vampire Book*; *The History Detectives Explore Lincoln's Letter, Parker's Sax, and Mark Twain's Watch: And Many More Mysteries of America's Past*; *The Everything® Pirates Book*; *The Everything® Freemasons Book*; and *The Everything® Filmmaking Book*. When not writing, Ms. Karg works as an editor, graphic designer, and layout specialist. She lives in the Pacific Northwest with her better half and writing partner, Rick Sutherland, and is currently at work on a vampire series.